Bible Study Series

Hebrews

Covenant of Faith
Part 1

Pat Wellman

Jeannie McCullough, Executive Editor

BEACON HILL PRESS
OF KANSAS CITY

Copyright 2006
by Beacon Hill Press of Kansas City and Wisdom of the Word

ISBN-13: 978-0-8341-2265-9
ISBN-10: 0-8341-2265-0

Printed in the United States of America

Cover Design: Darlene Filley

Library of Congress Cataloging-in-Publication Data

Wellman, Pat, 1930-
    Hebrews : covenant of faith / Pat Wellman ; Jeannie McCullough, executive editor.
        p. cm. — (Wisdom of the Word Bible study series)
    Includes bibliographical references.
    ISBN-13: 978-0-8341-2265-9 (v. 1 : pbk.)
    ISBN-10: 0-8341-2265-0 (v. 1 : pbk.)
    ISBN-13: 978-0-8341-2275-8 (v. 2 : pbk.)
    ISBN-10: 0-8341-2275-8 (v. 2 : pbk.)
    1. Bible. N.T. Hebrews—Textbooks. I. McCullough, Jeannie. II. Title. III. Series.

    BS2775.55.W45 2006
    227'.870071—dc22

                                                                                    2006013753

10   9   8   7   6   5   4   3   2   1

Contents

About Wisdom of the Word

Wisdom of the Word (W.O.W.) was founded in 1986 by Jeannie McCullough in Bethany, Oklahoma. It began as a weekly Bible study at Bethany First Church of the Nazarene. In the first year the study grew to over 400 members, and women from other churches and the community began joining. The local enrollment of Wisdom of the Word eventually exceeded 1,000 and has included men, women, and children of all ages and many denominations.

Wisdom of the Word has been an instrument in uniting the community of believers as well as reaching the unchurched and the lost. It is now ministering to thousands through videos and cassette tapes and other programs such as Children of the Word, prison ministries, and missions.

About the Name

W.O.W. began as "Women of the Word." Then when men began to join in the study with the women, the name was changed to "Wisdom of the Word," not only to retain the W.O.W. acronym but also to reflect the mission: to have our lives visible changed by gaining wisdom from God's Word and responding in radical obedience to His voice.

About Jeannie McCullough

Jeannie McCullough was a pastor's wife until June 2004. She is also a mother and grandmother. Her life and ministry have taken her to Bethany, Oklahoma, where her husband, Mel, served as senior pastor of Bethany First Church of the Nazarene. In June 2004 he accepted the position of inaugural president of the Nazarene Foundation, located in Olathe, Kansas, near Kansas City. Since that time they have been in transition between Oklahoma City and Kansas City. Jeannie understands firsthand how radical obedience to God's Word can change a life.

Southern Nazarene University granted Jeannie an honorary doctorate in 1997. Due to her humor and honesty as well as her unique insights and application of the Scriptures in daily living, she is in great demand as a speaker throughout North America. Jeannie strives to be a "salt tablet" who will make others thirst for God's Word. As she has committed herself to being a student of the Word, God has given her many opportunities to share what He is teaching her.

About the Author

PAT WELLMAN ministered for many years in Denver with her pastor husband, the late Donald Wellman. She has taught numerous Bible study groups, has spoken for various retreats, and is the author of three previous books. She admits that Hebrews is one of her favorite portions of Scripture. Pat now lives in Oklahoma City and has two children and six grandchildren.

Introduction to Hebrews

Bible students sometimes declare the Book of Hebrews very difficult to understand. And to some degree, that is true. It is possible that this is the reason it was not included in the canon of the Bible for many years. The word "canon" simply means an official list, a standard, or the rule by which something is judged. The Bible is comprised of a group of writings, or books, believed to be inspired by God.

Hebrews was recognized at the beginning as the work of a scholar written to a group of highly educated people, also scholars. Paul was regarded as both educated and a scholar, so some Bible historians believe that when Hebrews was first included as a book in the canon, it was only because it was thought to have been written by Paul. Almost immediately this conclusion came under attack, and modern theologians are almost unanimous in their belief that Paul was *not* its author.

Origen, a second-century theologian, said tongue-in-cheek, "It lacked the apostle's rudeness of expression."

E. F. Scott wrote, "The Epistle to the Hebrews is in many respects the riddle of the New Testament."[1] William Barclay commented, "When we ask when it was written, to whom it was written, and who wrote it, we can only guess and grope."[2]

Indeed, Hebrews is a more sophisticated text than the abrupt style of writing attributed to Paul. Its style more closely resembles the Greek works of scholars examining or embracing the "new" Christianity. Apollos, an educated and scholarly Jewish Christian, is still considered by many as its likely author. Yet though it may not resemble Paul's writing style, it most certainly teaches his bedrock theology.

It may just be that God chose to give us some of the greatest words of instruction and inspiration found in His Word without the identification of the writer in order to preserve unto himself the full message of the New Covenant: *Jesus is superior.*

H. Orton Wiley, noted modern theologian, reminds us that Hebrews is very much a commentary on the Old Testament. He writes, "It recounts the journey in the wilderness, the significance of the Tabernacle, and is an interpretation of the various offerings and services in the worship of ancient Israel. The Epistle begins, however, not with the twelfth, but with the twenty-fourth chapter of Exodus. . . . It is not concerned with what is represented by bringing Israel out of Egypt, but with what is meant by bringing them into the land of promise."[3]

This should be our emphasis. We are in the dispensation, or "time of," the Son. This is the "land of promise" for this century, and at no time has civilization needed the Jesus of Hebrews more. Referring to the letter to the Hebrews, Augustine pronounced, "The New is in the Old concealed, the Old is in the New revealed!" Christ came not to *invalidate* the message of the Old Testament but to *fulfill* its purpose and prophecy. God is establishing a new covenant. Dr. Wiley says, "This covenant (1) embraces the law of God written in the minds and hearts of His people . . . hearts so transformed that they are brought into perfect harmony with the will of God. (2) It embraces the remission of sins, which not only includes the pardon of actual transgressions, but the cleansing from 'inbred sin' or the 'carnal mind.'. . .

"(3) It exalts God as the supreme and sole object of worship and adoration, the heart being so purified that its affections are set on things above; its will, always obedient to the will of God; and its mind, the 'mind of Christ.'"[4] We can only shout, "Wow—and this is for us!

The date of the writing of Hebrews, though never definitely determined, is generally placed between A.D. 60 and A.D. 70. Two predominant reasons are as follows.

(1) In A.D. 70 Jerusalem and its Temple were both de-

As you begin each day, use this acrostic to help you study:

Wait *for the Holy Spirit to teach you as you read His Word.*

Obey *what God instructs you to do.*

Remember *to praise God for insights and promises fulfilled.*

Discover *for yourself the incredible faithfulness of God!*

stroyed by Rome. Hebrews includes many references to the sacrificial system of worship in the Temple but makes no mention of the destruction of this very center of Jewish worship. Evidently, the Temple was still standing at the time of the writing of Hebrews. Hebrews uses the present tense in speaking of these sacrifices, and since A.D. 70 the Jews have never had a place to offer their sacrifices.

(2) The old order of Jewish worship revolved around the Temple, and its destruction was regarded by the writer of Hebrews as God's coming judgment on that system. It would be very odd, had it taken place, for the writer not to have mentioned it.

The writer of Hebrews speaks to a group who had accepted Christ sometime earlier. In fact, they were mildly chastised because their growth had been slow.

Verse 12 of chapter 5 reads, *By this time you ought to be teachers.* They were contemplating a return to Judaism to escape the severe persecution taking place among Christian converts. The writer says strongly, *Remember those earlier days after you had received the light, when you stood your ground in a great contest in the face of suffering* (10:32). Through his own experience he declares Christ and Christianity superior to the Jewish prophets, the angels, Moses, Joshua, the Aaronic priesthood, Abraham, the Jewish high priesthood, the Old Testament covenant, the Tabernacle, the Levitical sacrifices, the promises of Judaism, and the Jewish law that points to Christ. For the Jew there was nothing left to compete with the Christ. Today we add emphatically that when you have Christ you have everything!

Contemporary language might shout, "What a package deal!" Welcome to joy everlasting.

All the theology of the Book of Hebrews should not frighten us away or make us hesitant to search its words for blessings and spiritual edification. Each of us will discover his or her own revelations. And each of us will find passages that are hard to understand. An open heart will go a long way toward making this book come alive. God always blesses an open heart in special ways.

Enjoy!

Bible Study Series

Hebrews

LESSON 1

■ **A Study of Hebrews 1:1-3**

God Speaks

Read Hebrews 1:1-3.

1. How did God speak to forefathers in the past?

2. The Bible records many times when God spoke to people. One example is found in Matthew 1:20-24.

   a. In verse 20, what agent did God use to speak to Joseph?

   b. Who declared the news reported in verse 23?

The coming of Christ, and His death and resurrection, changed forever God's method of salvation. With that change came a new message: salvation through the risen Christ. For the Hebrews, to whom the writer speaks, accepting this change was very difficult.

For most of us it's not easy to change traditions, habits, or beliefs, maybe because the old and familiar things seem "safe" to us. It's easy to think, *Why struggle with something new and different when what I know has been a way of life for so long?* It's comfortable. Familiar ground is often hallowed ground. Mom's kitchen is a comfortable place because it's there, hopefully, that we have felt secure. Even those who live in a not-so-traditional environment get attached to surroundings.

This difficulty to change can also be true with belief. People often find it easier to cling to a preconceived or inherited belief than to accept something new. It's wise for us to examine carefully anything new that affects our be-

lief or behavior. So it was with the Jews of the first century. Many who had accepted Jesus as the Messiah, Son of God, heir to all things, and comaker of the universe, were now struggling between the old and the new. Persecution was becoming very intense. For the first time, these Christian Jews found themselves confronted with a "once-and-for-all" decision.

The truth is that most Christian believers experience this process to some degree. Satan makes it his business to tempt us to turn away, maybe more than once. So the Hebrews writer begins the book saying to the new believers that God has always "spoken," in many ways, to lead us to His truth. And let's be careful to listen.

3. List some of the ways God speaks to people today.

   a. What does He speak about?

   b. When and how did He first speak to you?

Hebrews 1:1 says, *In the past God spoke to our forefathers.* God has always made himself known.

Isaiah 40:8

The grass withers and the flowers fall, but the word of our God stands forever.

4. Complete John 1:18: _____ _____ has ever
   _____ God, but God the _____ _____, who is
   the _____ _____, has made him
   _____.

The Hebrews writer, from the very beginning of the book, knew it was important to say that this new gospel was a continuation of the Old Testament. He also knew it was very important to say that God is very anxious to communicate truth to us. Romans 10:17 tells us how the God of the New Testament would accomplish this: *Faith comes from hearing the message, and the message is heard through the word of Christ.* The message and faith *go* and *grow* together!

It is so important for us to learn to recognize God's voice. Sometimes He speaks through His Word. Sometimes He speaks through a conversation we might have with another Christian. He speaks in various ways, but without a doubt the most meaningful times are when He speaks to us directly. 1 Timothy 4:1 begins with the words, *The Spirit clearly says . . .*

5. Read Hebrews 12:24-25, and record the first sentence of verse 25.

The following words are taken from Psalm 19:7-8: *The law of the Lord is perfect. . . . The statutes of the Lord are trustworthy. . . . The precepts of the Lord are right. . . . The commands of the Lord are radiant.* It is through this law, these statutes and precepts, that God is so anxious to speak to us. He also will personalize them for each of us if we will but ask and listen!

DAY TWO

God Speaks Through His Son

Read Hebrews 1:1-3.

1. According to verse 2, how does God speak to us today?

The last days mentioned in verse 2 are not those just before the Great Judgment. This refers to the last of the "days" or periods of prophecy just before the fulfillment of the promise, which was the coming of the Son. God appointed His Son heir of all things, through whom He made the universe.

2. List the descriptions of Christ found in Hebrews 1:1-3.

3. Read John 16:33. Following these words, Jesus began praying. His prayer is recorded in the next chapter, John 17. Copy the first two sentences of His prayer.

What does this tell us about the relationship between the Father and the Son?

It is this oneness of the Father and Son that prompted God the Father to send the Son to earth. The Father had utmost confidence in His Son to carry out the plan of salvation. John in his Gospel refers many times to this Father-Son oneness and the work they do together.

4. *a.* Record John 10:30.

   b. Record John 14:6.

5. The Father speaks through His Son, and the Son obeys! Jesus affirms this by His words of John 14:31:

The world must _____ that I _____ the _____ and that I do _____ what my Father has _____ me.

What an example for us as God's children!

6. What were Christ's responsibilities as Son?

   a. Matthew 11:27

   b. John 5:19-20

   c. John 17:1

The early Christians needed to be taught the unique relationship between God and Jesus in order to accept the fact that God could and would speak through His Son.

God had spoken through the prophets. The prophets each wrote their message through the "eyeglasses" of their own experiences.

- Amos cried for social justice because he lived in such an unfair world
- Isaiah wanted God's holiness
- Hosea, because of his own sad home life, was inspired by God's forgiving love.

Now in the New Testament, God sends His Son and speaks to all of humanity through Him.

We, too, have our own "eyeglasses" with which to see Jesus. Some see Him as the Good Shepherd; others cherish Him as Redeemer the most.

7. *a.* List all the names of Jesus, the Son, that come to mind. (Don't worry if you're a new Christian and your list is short.)

   b. Put a star beside one or two that are your favorites. Do you know why these are special?

In Matthew's Gospel, at the beginning of chapter 17, we find an account of what is called the Transfiguration. Jesus took Peter, James, and John to a mountain by themselves, and here Jesus was transfigured (changed to His glorified being) before them.

8. In verse 5 the Father speaks from the heavens. He makes three very important statements. The first two are recorded below. Write in the third.
   This is my Son, whom I love.
   With him I am well pleased.
   _____ _____ _____!

God speaks to us through His Son! Ask Him today to speak to you about something you are concerned about. If you feel comfortable doing so, write your request and His answer in your Bible.

MEMORY CHALLENGE

The grass _____ and the _____ fall, but the _____ of our _____ stands forever.
                                                        Isaiah 40:8

The Glorious Radiance

Read Hebrews 1:3.

1. Because Jesus is the radiance of God's glory, He is superior to all others. Several times this is recorded in the Book of Hebrews. After each reference write who or what He is superior to:

   1:4-6

   3:3

   4:8

   5:1-10

   8:6

   10:8-10

2. *a.* From a dictionary record the definition of "radiance."

   b. From the same dictionary list words or phrases found under "radiant."

3. The Father and the Son are one. Jesus radiates all that the Father is. He is—

   Leviticus 19:1 _____

   Deuteronomy 7:9 _____

   Deuteronomy 7:21 _____

   2 Chronicles 30:9 _____

   Luke 18:19 _____

   Romans 11:22 _____

   1 John 4:16 _____

4. Furthermore, all that Jesus is, so is the Father!

a. John 6:35 says Jesus is _____

   _____ _____ _____. So is
   God the Father.

b. John 8:12 says Jesus is _____

   _____ _____
   _____. So is God the Father.

c. John 14:6 says Jesus is _____

   _____ _____ _____
   _____ _____ _____
   _____. So is God the Father.

The life of Jesus on earth was a reflection of the Father. The nature of both the Father and Son are identical. God wants us to know the radiance of both the Father and the Son through His Spirit.

But much more than that, God the Father and God the Son long for us to be the radiance of their glory. This is really the most effective way we serve God.

Perhaps the writer of Hebrews realized his readers struggled with this profound truth. It's helpful to know the disciples struggled with it as well.

5. Read in John 14:8-9 Jesus' response to Philip's request just before His crucifixion and death. Record His reply:

6. Read in Colossians 1:15-20 Paul's words about Jesus. Record the first part of verse 15.

7. Record Ephesians 5:1.

We are blind to the light of God until He, in Christ, shines on us. Others may be blind to the light of God until He shines *through* us.

8. Choose one of the following:

   a. Be the "radiance" to someone today by a note, phone call, or word of encouragement.

   b. Write a note of appreciation to someone who has been the radiance (or reflection) of Christ to you.

MEMORY CHALLENGE

Print the memory verse in the middle of a sizeable piece of paper. Draw withered grass and fallen flowers around it. Put it on a cupboard door or on the refrigerator.

DAY FOUR

Jesus, the Representative

Reread Hebrews 1:3.

1. Write the phrase that relates to today's title.

Jesus is not just a "likeness" of God the Father. He is more than that. He is *one with* the Father. This oneness is vital to the plan of salvation, which is provided for us by the death and resurrection of Jesus. That is a concept not always easy to understand.

Spiritual truth must be grounded on what God says and accepted by faith. That's what makes it of the "Spirit."

2. Why do we sometimes have difficulty accepting what we cannot physically "see"?

The author of Hebrews wrote to a group who evidently were very well versed in their knowledge of God the Father. Now the writer says it is time for them to see and accept the fact that Jesus, God's Son, is the Father's "representative."

3. Read John 10:30, 37.

   a. Verse 30 says, _____ and the _____ are _____.

   b. Verse 37 says, *Do not* _____ *me unless I* _____ *what my* _____ *does.*

   c. Now read verse 38. If these Hebrews did not want to believe Jesus, what did He say they could believe to prove that He and the Father were one?

Hebrews 1:3 says that Christ is the exact representation of His (the Father's) *being*. In the Greek language this was the word used to describe the engraved image of a seal or stamp. This was the way any document was made official. The Greek word for "representation" meant *exact replica*, as found in a seal transferred by wax. If the process was done properly, the original and the wax impression were interchangeable, even for legal purposes. Just as Christ bears the Father's "stamp," we should bear Christ's stamp of righteous behavior.

4. Read the following scriptures aloud, saying the word "exact" before the word "image." Then write your favorite phrase from the following selections.

   • 2 Corinthians 4:4

   • Colossians 1:15

   • Colossians 3:9-10

5. Our desire and goal as Christians should be to be the "exact representation" of Jesus. With that in mind, list some things you think the "world" looks for and expects from Christians.

6. Read aloud Philippians 2:5-11. Record verse 11.

To be like Christ includes living as He did. We acknowledge, of course, that we are not divine as He is. But we must not use that as an excuse. Yes, we have "warts," so to speak, but if we give ourselves to being like Him, we will allow Him to work with us. "To be like Christ" includes living as He directs us, allowing Him to make us *His* exact representation, to have patience and diligence to be like Him! And we do not have to be "perfect" before He can use us to be His "exact representation."

One of the most humbling experiences of my life still affects me deeply whenever I think about it. It came after a very long period of time I spent trying to get a young mother to understand what and who God is and how much He loved her and wanted her as His born-again child. She was from another country, spoke another language, and had never heard about salvation through Jesus. As she began to understand English, I explained everything about God I could think of. I read about Him from His Word. I told her what was necessary for salvation and how Jesus paid the price to make that salvation available to us. I tried to nourish a desire to know about Him into an actual experience with Him. I explained "grace" and His availability. Nothing! After more than a year, I found myself worn out with the challenge.

Very late one evening, I answered my phone to hear her excited voice. "I know God!" she said. Before I could ask how and why, she said, "I realized that if you could know God, then *I could know Him!* And so I asked Him into my heart!" How humbling to be God's representative to mirror His image! Humbling, scary—and possible! And I was no longer weary!

MEMORY CHALLENGE

Close your eyes, say the memory verse, and try to imagine "forever."

The Power of His Word

Read Hebrews 1:1-3.

1. *a.* Who spoke God's Word in the past?

   b. Who does God speak through *in these last days?*

2. What is meant by the phrase "I give you my word"?

God's Word is exactly that, *His* Word. It is not a copy, a translation, or quotations from other sources. He has protected His Word and makes it known to those who will listen. In the *New International Version* Isaiah 55:11 reads, *My word . . . will not return to me empty.* In this case, however, the King James Version is probably closer to the actual meaning: *My word . . . shall not return unto me void.* Here the word "void" does not mean a void as in a vacuum or a huge empty space. The proper meaning is that it (His Word) shall not be canceled, stamped out, or found worthless.

As we have noted earlier in this study, the beginning words of Hebrews tell us that God spoke through the prophets, but in this passage we note that He speaks by His Son and sustains His Word through Him. The prophets were vessels or channels to proclaim God. Jesus, the Son, *is* God.

3. The closing phrase of verse 3 says, *[He is] sustaining all things by his powerful word.*

   a. Using a dictionary, copy the meaning of the word "sustain."

   b. Copy the meaning of the word "powerful."

4. Look at Genesis 1:1-26.

   a. Record the beginning words of verses 3, 6, 9, 11, 14, 24.

   b. What were the amazing results of God's speaking?

5. Jesus did not need to repeat himself when speaking to the forces of nature. Nature responded to His Word without hesitation. One example of this is in Matthew 8:26. Record it here.

6. Throughout the Bible, the forces of nature respond instantly to God's Word. We would do well to do so also. Realizing the truth of the following references should help us to do that. The Bible says God's Word is—

   Psalm 19:7 _____

   Psalm 19:8 _____

   Psalm 111:7 _____

   Psalm 111:8 _____

   Philippians 2:16 _____

7. Read 1 Peter 1:23-25. What are the words or phrases that refer to God's Word?

8. The following verses of Psalm 119 begin with two- or three-word requests for God's involvement in the psalmist's life through His Word. Record them.

   Verse 33:

   Verse 34:

   Verse 35:

   Verse 36:

   William Barclay writes, "If the writer to the Hebrews had one text and one summons, it was 'Let us draw near!'"[1] His Word will always move us closer!

9. Recall a specific time when God spoke to you through His Word and how that helped you. Share this experience with someone. It will encourage you both!

Ask a family member or friend to define "forever."

DAY SIX

The Intercessor

Read Hebrews 1:1-3.

1. Jesus came to earth with an assignment. According to verse 3, what was it?

The writer of Hebrews has described Jesus, the Son, in several carefully detailed ways. In review, note these seven descriptive statements:
- Heir of all things
- Maker of the universe
- The radiance of God's glory
- The exact representation of the Father's being
- He sustains all things.
- He provides purification for our sins.
- He sits at the right hand of God. His authority comes as a result of His sacrificial death. It is here that He intercedes for us.

The "intercessor" is exactly what Jesus is in the "administrative" duties of the Trinity. We should remind ourselves that we are not capable of completely understanding the "three-in-one" Godhead. In part, that is because we live in a world of individuals and individual things. The Trinity (Father, Son, Holy Spirit) existing as one is hard for us to grasp. Also, the Bible makes it clear that each member of the Trinity has His own work and responsibility. We can and should praise the Three-in-One for their work in our lives even though we cannot completely understand it. Remember, *faith* is the basis of our walk with God.

2. A very interesting mention of the Three-in-One occurs in the very beginning of the Bible.

   a. Record the first 10 words of Genesis 1:1.

   b. Now record the first 13 words of Genesis 1:26.

   c. What difference do you see?

   d. What does this indicate to us?

3. Read Matthew 3:16-17. Each member of the Trinity was involved here. What was each doing?

   a. Father _____

   b. Son _____

   c. Holy Spirit _____

4. Who is referred to in the following scriptures, and what does each do?

   Romans 8:26

   Romans 8:31-32

   Romans 8:34

Isn't it a comfort to know that the Son, the Savior, intercedes for us? He has direct access to God the Father. He knows what we need to be victorious Christians!

Theologians say there are four basic concepts or ideas that form the religions of the world. As we finish this introductory passage from Hebrews 1:1-3, let's look at them and see where Christ, the superior one, "fits."

There is the possibility of fellowship with "a god" —just a possibility.

A system or discipline gives us a standard for life and the power to reach that standard; we become good by self-improvement or, using a modern term, humanism.

Religion is actually the highest achievement of the mind. Knowledge is king, and understanding is supreme.

In the Bible Paul says there is a great experience that is absolutely available: Christ in me, and I in Christ.

Both James and Peter address this: James 1:5 says, *If any of you lacks wisdom, he should ask God.* 1 Peter 1:13 says, *Prepare your minds for action; be self-controlled; set your hope fully on the grace to be given you when Jesus Christ is revealed.*

John 1:18 declares, *No one has ever seen God, but God the One and Only, who is at the Father's side, has made him known.*

There is direct access to God! This should be the most exciting definition for us as Christians. The religions of the world offer lots of opinions about how this can be. With great discussion, they explore the "who," "what," and "how."

This is exactly what the writer of Hebrews tells us.

5. The Book of Hebrews has a great deal to say about the "who." Jesus' crucifixion and death provided the way of salvation. He wants to be involved in every day of our lives. Hebrews 7:25 is one of the most important verses ever written. Record it here.

Each day this week begin or end your prayer time with *Thank you, Jesus, for interceding for me!*

MEMORY CHALLENGE

Recite the verse, and ask God to remind you often of the "foreverness" of His Word.

Hebrews

■ A Study of Hebrews 1:4-9

DAY ONE

The Superiority of the Son: His Name

Read Hebrews 1:4-9.

1. Read Hebrews 1:4. Jesus inherited His name. To whom is He superior?

Jesus, the Son, is not just superior. He holds a place none other has ever held. He is the Son of the Godhead. *He is God!* This is said so beautifully by Paul in Colossians 1:15-18—

He is the image of the invisible God, the firstborn over all creation. For by him all things were created: things in heaven and on earth, visible and invisible, whether thrones or powers or rulers or authorities; all things were created by him and for him. He is before all things, and in him all things hold together. And he is the head of the body, the church; he is the beginning and the firstborn from among the dead, so that in everything he might have the supremacy.

Jesus himself confirmed His preexistence and superiority: "*I tell you the truth,*" *Jesus answered,* "*before Abraham was born, I am!*" (John 8:58).

Two groups were evidently very important to the receivers of the Hebrews letter: the prophets and the angels. We cannot read the Bible without recognizing the existence and prominence of both. Keeping in mind that Hebrews was addressed to a specific body of believers, we can conclude that angels played a significant role in their lives. Perhaps they believed that Jesus, the Son, was not as important as the angels, did not have as much power as

the angels, or that He himself was an angel. But the Bible clearly says that the angels were subordinate to Jesus, the Son. Hebrews declares that even His name is superior to that of the angels.

Previously in this study we looked at Hebrews 1:3. There we find a phrase describing Christ as *the exact representation of his [God's] being.* Literally, it means that He is the expression of God's character. His very name suggests and reflects that.

2. Record the names of Christ in these scriptures:

John 6:51

Revelation 1:5

Revelation 19:13

No other name compares to the name of Jesus. And special results often accompany His name.

3. What is said about His name in the following references?

Matthew 1:21

Matthew 1:23

The angels were great in the eyes of the Hebrews, but Hebrews 1 declares that angels did not merit being above the Son, nor could they be a valid comparison. They had an exalted position. Some were at the throne of God. They

---

MEMORY CHALLENGE

Revelation 4:8

Holy, holy, holy is the Lord God Almighty, who was, and is, and is to come.

were at home in heaven. They possessed a holy character. However, they were created; Jesus the Son was *begotten*.

4. Philippians 2:9-11 says that God exalted the Son and gave Him a name that is superior so that—

    a. Record verse 10:

    b. Record verse 11:

    Psalm 103:20 says the angels must praise the Lord. At the beginning of the same psalm, David says in exaltation, *Praise the LORD, O my soul; all my inmost being, praise his holy name* (verse 1). This is our privilege. However, in the New Testament, Timothy reminds us that claiming the holy name demands appropriate behavior: *Everyone who confesses the name of the Lord must turn away from wickedness* (2 Timothy 2:19).

5. Record the names given to the Son in Isaiah 9:6.

6. Read Psalm 9:10. Knowing His name means _____ Him!

    For centuries Christians who have claimed His name have looked forward to His coming back to earth. Though no one knows when that will be, we do have a description of this event beginning in Revelation 19:11. And when He comes, He will bear the greatest name of all, not applicable to the angels. *On his robe and on his thigh he has this name written: KING OF KINGS AND LORD OF LORDS* (Revelation 19:16).

> The name of Jesus is so sweet,
> I love its music to repeat.
> It makes my joy full and complete,
> The precious name of Jesus!
>
> I love the name of Him whose heart
> Knows all my griefs and bears a part,
> Who bids all anxious fears depart—
> I love the name of Jesus!
>
> .   .   .   .
>
> No word of man can ever tell
> How sweet the name I love so well.
> Oh, let its praises ever swell!
> Oh, praise the name of Jesus!
> —W. C. Martin

The Father-Son Relationship

Read Hebrews 1:5.

1. What is the relationship between God and Jesus in today's scripture?

    As soon as Jesus was baptized, he went up out of the water. At that moment heaven was opened, and he saw the Spirit of God descending like a dove and lighting on him. And a voice from heaven said, "This is my Son, whom I love; with him I am well pleased" (Matthew 3:16-17).

    In any relationship with God the Father there must be the acknowledgement that Jesus is the Son and that He and the Father are one. In our minds we tend to separate them, but any description of God in His Word is also one of Jesus, His Son.

2. After each of the following references, state the role given to God:

    Psalm 96:13

    Isaiah 40:10

    Isaiah 40:11

    Isaiah 40:25-26

3. Read Genesis 49:22-25.

    a. What are the three titles given in verse 24?

    b. Record the name in verse 25.

4. With God's Word we can build a profile of the interchangeable nature that is found in both the Father and the Son.

    God the Father is—
    Deuteronomy 33:27

Nehemiah 9:17

Job 37:22

John 4:24

Jesus the Son is—
John 10:14

Ephesians 2:20

Colossians 1:15

Colossians 1:16

5. Read John 5:17. What does this verse suggest about the Father-Son relationship?

6. Read John 8:17-19.
   a. Record the question in the first part of verse 19.

   b. Record the answer in the second part of verse 19.

Because we do not experience oneness in the sense that the Holy Trinity does, it is hard for us to totally understand what it is and how it works. Therefore, it takes faith to accept that the Father, Son, and Holy Spirit are one. Faith is at the heart of our salvation!

7. Read John 6:38-40.
   a. Why did Jesus come from heaven?

   b. What is the Father's will for Him?

> *My God is reconciled;*
> *His pardoning voice I hear.*
> *He owns me for His child;*
> *I can no longer fear.*
> *With confidence I now draw nigh,*
> *With confidence I now draw nigh,*
> *And "Father, Abba Father," cry.*
> *—Charles Wesley*

MEMORY CHALLENGE

Write the memory verse on a piece of paper, and clip it to the cover of your Bible for this week's study.

DAY THREE

Superior to the Angels

Read Hebrews 1:5-6.

1. What is the relationship between the Son and angels in today's passage?

Although the Old Testament contains many references to the duties of angels, they are sometimes called by other names.

2. Read each of the following scriptures, and summarize the function of the angels involved:

   Joshua 5:13-15

   2 Kings 19:35

   Isaiah 6:1-3

   Daniel 6:19-22

"She [He] is such an angel!" These words spoken today are usually describing a very giving, gentle person who comes to the rescue of, or provides for the needs of, another person. "Angels" are those who minister to us in very meaningful, often surprising ways. Certainly all of us need these types of people, and most of us can identify one or more in our lives.

However, the angels of both testaments of the Bible are very different from that, both in purpose and administration. In the Greek and Hebrew languages the word for "angel" means "messenger," or "agent," someone acting on the part of a higher being. They were very prominent in the ancient religions. All the various systems of belief had a "sovereign" who, in turn, had a messenger or agent. As the earth's population grew, the belief was that the sovereign could not communicate with all its subjects, so messengers of the "deity" became necessary to reach all the people.

The belief was soon established that this was what angels were for—to communicate between the "god" and humans. William Barclay commented on this subject:

> Men felt more and more the distance and the difference between God and man. They felt that God was ever farther and farther away and more and more unknowable and unreachable. . . . In the Old Testament the law was given directly by God to Moses. . . . But in New Testament times the Jews believed that God gave the law first to angels and that angels passed it on to Moses because direct communication between man and God was unthinkable.[1]

By the first century, angels had risen in the minds of people to great power and authority and were indispensable.

In Hebrews 1 the writer makes it clear that the angels are inferior to the Son and are not spoken of in the same manner of God the Father. No doubt the writer was aware of how important angels had become to the theology of the Jews and thought it important to say that they were also a part of the new faith of Christianity.

The Jews also believed that when God said in Genesis 1:26, *Let* us *make man . . .* (emphasis added), He was talking to the angels and including them in the creative genius of God. Of course, God was actually referring to the Trinity. But those who insisted on great importance for angels began to develop a system that by New Testament times had designated angels for hundreds of things and situations. According to a Rabbinic saying, "Every blade of grass has its angels." So knowing the makeup and background of his readers, the Hebrews writer recognized the critical importance of declaring the Son superior to the angels.

3. *a.* In Hebrews 1:6 God says to let _____ _____ _____ worship the Son.

   b. Who else worships Him?

   Matthew 2:1-2

   Matthew 28:16-17

   John 9:30-38

Angels are mentioned often in both testaments of the Bible. They know about the activities of God's kingdom and are referred to in many circumstances.

4. Read 1 Peter 3:21-22:

   The angels are in _____ to _____.

5. *a.* How would you summarize the reply of the angel as recorded in Revelation 22:8-9?

b. What are the two very important words at the end of verse 9 of that passage?

Adam Clarke wrote, "To worship any creature is idolatry, and God resents idolatry more than any other evil. Jesus Christ can be no creature, else the angels who worship him must be guilty of idolatry, and God the author of that idolatry, who commanded those angels to worship Christ."[2]

Bottom line: Angels are special and important. But we must remember that *nothing* should be of more importance to us than Jesus or worshiped in any way. *Jesus is superior.*

MEMORY CHALLENGE

Read the verse quietly five times. Then say it without the printed copy.

The Nature of His Kingdom

Read Hebrews 1:7-8.

1. What four important nouns about the Son are used in Hebrews 1:8?

2. Record Psalm 45:6-7.

Theologians call Hebrews 1:8 a messianic passage, meaning it refers to the Messiah and the coming kingdom of the Savior. The Hebrews writer has left no doubt that two things are true: (1) the Son has a divine throne but the angels do not and (2) the Son is Lord, while angels are His subjects. Having established the superiority of the Son over the angels and their work, the writer now establishes the divinity of His being by quoting the Psalms passage. He continues to quote God the Father, who in verse 8 calls His Son *God.* The Son does not need to prove His lineage or line of command, because God has proclaimed the eternal throne and kingdom of His Son. And His scepter (trademark) will be righteousness.

A throne has always been the symbol of authority and kingship. It presupposes a kingdom, however small or large, that is subject to the one occupying the throne. Of course, history reminds us that the "power" on the throne is not always a just one. This is not so in the kingdom of heaven. The standard by which a throne should be judged is found in Proverbs 16:12—*A throne is established through righteousness.*

3. Fill in the blanks from the following verses of scripture:

   The _____ reigns _____; _____ has established his throne for _____ (Psalm 9:7).

   The _____ is on his _____ _____. He _____ the sons of men; his eyes _____ them (Psalm 11:4).

   None other except Jesus qualifies to claim this throne. Matthew has several observations concerning this throne. Write in the missing words:

   I tell you, _____ _____ _____ _____ _____: either by _____, _____ _____ is God's throne (Matthew 5:34).

   When the Son of Man comes in his glory, and all the angels with him, he will _____ on _____ _____ in _____ _____. All the _____ will be gathered before Him (Matthew 25:31-32a).

4. Jesus has a rightful, promised place on the throne in God's kingdom. Read Acts 2:29-30.

   a. Who does Peter say God made a promise to?

   b. What was that promise?

   You may trace the fulfillment of this promise by reading Matthew 1:1-17.

   The throne is definitely a part of the heavenly scene. Micaiah wrote in 2 Chronicles 18:18, *Hear the word of the LORD: I saw the LORD sitting on his throne with all the host of heaven standing on his right and on his left.*

   John in his Gospel makes a statement concerning the activity of judgment from the throne.

5. Record John 5:22.

   In ancient times, to be allowed to be in the presence of the throne and its inhabitant was very rare and usually very dangerous. In most incidents a person was there to be sentenced or punished. Today we still have thrones and monarchs in our world, and proper behavior and dress are still demanded regardless of the occasion.

6. Imagine yourself in one of the throne rooms, approaching the ruler who sits on the throne with scepter in hand.

   a. What do you think you would be feeling and thinking?

   b. Record Hebrews 4:16.

   Various definitions are offered for "scepter," summarized by "a rod or staff carried to denote royal power or authority." The purpose of the scepter is to show who represents the kingdom. Monarchs and kings of the ancient world carried a rod or spearlike shaft that bore the seal and symbol of their rule.

7. In the Bible the power of the scepter was demonstrated several times. Let's look at examples:

   • Read Isaiah 14:3-5. What signaled the fall of Babylon?

   This action meant Babylon had lost its identification.

   • Read Zechariah 10:11. What describes the fall of Egypt?

In the beautiful story from the Old Testament book of Esther, King Xerxes chose Esther as queen. But even in her exalted position, she could not enter his presence without being summoned to do so. At this time the Jews were about to be killed, and Mordecai, a Jew, insisted that Esther, herself a Jew, plead the plight of the Jews before the king. So frightening was this assignment that Esther and her maids fasted for three days and nights. In both her appearances before the king, she was proclaimed worthy to be there by the extension of the king's scepter, which was God's answer to prayer and the deliverance of the Jews.

My trip to Egypt was one of the most unusual experiences of my life. It was, as they say, a "mixed bag." I loved its history but hated the poverty. I loved its historic grandeur but hated its spiritual bondage. At the Museum of Cairo I saw centuries of history displayed in art, relics, furniture, and statues: all remnants of great regimes and wealth. One large section honored King Tut. His symbol, the serpent, decorated his many chariots, thrones, robes, jewels—everything. His scepters, all bearing a likeness of a serpent, decorated walls, tables, and glass cases. Here was displayed in age-old artifacts testimony to great power. But—he was dead!

As I walked out the massive doors, my heart began to sing! I found myself praising God. I said to myself, *Jesus, my Savior, sits on an everlasting throne. His scepter is righteousness, His kingdom peace—and He is alive! Hallelujah!*

MEMORY CHALLENGE

Recite the verse as the beginning of your prayers today.

DAY FIVE

Righteousness and the Kingdom

Read Hebrews 1:8-9.

1. What has God loved and hated?

2. *a.* Record Proverbs 4:23.

   b. Record Proverbs 27:19.

   c. Read Matthew 12:34-35. How would you express this in your own words?

At the heart of God's kingdom is righteousness. God is a holy and righteous God; therefore, He insists on a righteous kingdom. In the English language "righteous" can be used as either a noun or an adjective. Examples: In the sentence "The righteous shall inherit the kingdom" it is used as a noun, the subject of the verb phrase "shall inherit." In the sentence "God's kingdom is a righteous one" it is used as an adjective, describing "one," which in turn refers to "kingdom." Adding "-ness" to this word creates "righteousness," which is what a righteous person exhibits in his or her life.

Being righteous is a state or condition of the inner person. Righteousness is the product of that condition. Stating it another way, "righteous" is being without guilt before God, and righteousness is the evidence of that relationship. So we may rightfully say that the Christian, the born-again person, will reflect the nature of the Kingdom by the fruit that flows from the inner self. One of the many consistent themes from Genesis to Revelation is that God is righteous. Additionally, righteousness is the trademark of His kingdom. Nothing but righteousness can abide in His kingdom.

3. It is not making too much of these two words to say that unbelievers expect righteousness from the righteous. Read 1 John 2:28-29, and record verse 29.

Verse 9 of today's passage says that Christ, *the Son*, loves righteousness. This righteousness is based on Christ's character, which hates wickedness. Some writers say that the degree of love and righteousness in the heart determines the lack, in proportion, of hate and wickedness.

4. Fill in the following blanks from Psalm 19:7-9:

   The _____ of the LORD *is _____* (verse 7).

   The result: _____

   The _____ of the LORD *are _____*
   (verse 7).

   The result: _____

   The _____ of the LORD *are _____* (verse 8).

   The result: _____

   The _____ of the LORD *are _____* (verse 8).

   The result: _____

   The _____ of the LORD *is _____, enduring _____. The ordinances of the* LORD *are _____ and _____ _____* (verse 9).

Verse 10 is a descriptive and inspiring challenge: *They are more precious than gold, than much pure gold; they are sweeter than honey, than honey from the comb.*

Paul wrote so many great and inspiring admonitions. Philippians 1:9-11 is a very special one: *This is my prayer: that your love may abound more and more in knowledge and depth of insight, so that you may be able to discern what is best and may be pure and blameless until the day of Christ, filled with the fruit of righteousness that comes through Jesus Christ—to the glory and praise of God.* A scepter (trademark) indeed!

Physicians who deal with the health of the human mind strongly emphasize the need for a person to find a "code" of behavior, or a standard by which to shape his or her life. The teachings of Jesus are of the highest value in providing that for us. It may be trite to say that His kingdom offers exactly what we need, but it is certainly true. We must actively pursue His kingdom.

5. Read Matthew 6:33. What two things should we desire to have?

   1. _____

   2. _____

E. Stanley Jones, best-selling author and lecturer, wrote, "Man needs nothing so much as he needs something upon which he can put his whole weight down in time and in eternity, something which will not turn sour or stale through sickness, old age, or death and which will give him something to sing about when there is nothing outwardly to sing about, nothing except the fact of an Unshakable Kingdom and an Unchanging Person."[1]

6. Read 2 Peter 1:10-11. The "things" mentioned here refer back to the inward qualities the writer has just listed in verses 5-7.

   a. There are seven things we should add to our faith. List them.

   b. It continues: *If you do these things, you will _____ _____* (verse 10).

7. Record Daniel 7:14.

MEMORY CHALLENGE

Write your own definition of "holy."

The Oil of Joy

Read Hebrews 1:9.

1. How has God set His Son above His companions?

2. Read Leviticus 21:10-12. Verses 10-11 prohibited the high priest from doing several things. Verse 12 tells why. What is that reason?

3. In the well-known Psalm 23, David rejoices in all the wonderful privileges found in the Lord. In verse 5 he lists two reasons He knows God cares for him. What are they?

One of the most meaningful items in my home is a wall plaque that reads, "Joy is peace . . . laughing!" If we look only at the life Jesus led and eventually gave for all of us, we may wonder about the peace He spoke of when He said in John 14:27, *Peace I leave with you; my peace I give you.* But He set a tremendous example for us: His peace and His joy are both products of His righteousness. Hebrews 1:9 says that God the Father rewarded Jesus the Son in a twofold way: by setting Him above His companions and all who had ever existed and by anointing Him with the oil of joy.

In the Bible "oil" is spoken of many times to signify a special blessing, approval, or the setting-apart of an individual for special duties. For example, the Book of Leviticus gives God's instructions to the Israelites for ordaining their priests. A very important part of the ceremony was the anointing with oil. Chapter 8 records the anointing of Aaron with oil as part of the ceremony making him a priest. Throughout the years the priests used oil in many different ways to signify different blessings.

It is fitting, then, that when God the Father demonstrates His love and appreciation for the Son, He does so by this very important and meaningful gesture: anointing Him with oil. And it is the oil of joy, or, as some translators say, *gladness.* How Jesus deserved some gladness!

4. Isaiah prophesied often about the promised Messiah. Record the first sentence of Isaiah 53:3.

Jesus came to end the reign of sin and suffering. He came to change the sadness of suffering into the oil of joy. God the Father seems to love the positive. Isaiah, the great prophet, was instructed to change the subject of his preaching.

5. Read Isaiah 61:1-3. Fill in the blanks from verse 3:
   - _____ _____ _____ _____ *instead of* _____
   - *the* _____ _____ _____ *instead of* _____
   - *and a garment of* _____ *instead of a* _____ _____ _____

In the fifth chapter of Galatians the apostle Paul writes of the great freedom available to the believer in Christ. He cautions, however, that there is no place for freedom of sinful behavior. Rather, the life of the Spirit is characterized by very specific attitudes. Galatians 5:22 lists the fruit that should be evident in the one living in the Spirit. Joy is one of them. We must remember that a fruit is a product of some other thing: a tree, plant, vine, or so on. From Jesus we received, among other things, *joy.*

6. Record Romans 14:17.

God anoints His children with the oil of joy and gladness. To those who do not know Christ, nothing is more attractive than that spirit of joy. The world should see this in believers!

A few years ago, Joy, a friend of mine, chose the word "joyful" for the insignia on her license plate. One day on her way to work she was stopped by a police officer. Thinking she was about to get a ticket, she reached for her billfold. "No," said the policeman, "I just want you to explain your license tag." She explained that her name was Joy but went on to say that the deeper meaning was that she was a born-again Christian and that Jesus Christ had given her great joy. Joy in Him was the most important thing about her life. She explained the way of salvation, and the officer listened intently. As he left, his "Have a great day!" was already a reality. She had given to another individual the possibility of the "anointing with oil" that comes from Jesus Christ, himself anointed by the Father. Could it be that the oil of gladness is our most effective testimony? Try it—you'll like it!

Pray that God will keep you mindful of His holiness.

Hebrews

LESSON 3

■ **A Study of Hebrews 1—2**

The Eternal Son

Read Hebrews 1:10—2:4.

People, places, and things are all woven into the fabric of our lives. In *The Sound of Music* Julie Andrews sang about "a few of my favorite things." We possess many, many things, and some of them are treasured. But the Bible teaches us that all things, as well as the human body, will die out and disappear. As William Shakespeare wrote, "All that lives must die, passing through nature to eternity" —a sobering fact.

Eternity is very difficult for us to genuinely understand. We know it means forever and ever and ever, but because everything we know about will have an ending, eternity is something we find hard to imagine.

The World Book Dictionary defines "eternal" as "independent of time conditions."[1] How very well that describes Jesus the Son! He was, and now is, independent of any of the time restrictions we live with. In today's verses God says of His Son that He was before the beginning and laid the foundations of our earth. The heavens are a result of His hand. Jesus was before all else and will be forever; He will never end. As some might say, "That's pretty heavy stuff!"

1. Record the second part of Hebrews 1:12 and 1 John 2:17 as one paragraph.

2. *a.* Fill in the blanks from Colossians 1:16—
   By him all things were _____: things in _____ and on _____, _____ and _____, whether thrones or powers or rulers or authorities; all things were created by him and for him.

   b. Record Colossians 1:17.

Today's verses from Hebrews are a direct quote from Psalm 102:25-27. Again we see the Hebrews writer reminding his readers of the Old Testament scriptures. The writer of Psalm 102 is unknown. But he was very familiar with the eternity of God and God's creation of the universe. He was someone suffering in Babylon, mourning over his own afflictions as well as those of his nation. The eternal nature of God was his comfort.

3. Read Numbers 23:19.

   a. List four things God will not do.

Titus 3:5

He saved us, not because of righteous things we had done, but because of his mercy.

b. Why should these verses be a comfort to us all?

4. Record the last sentence of 1 Corinthians 7:31.

The Bible speaks of the end of all things. We hear a lot today about the end of the world. We know prophecy says that this time will come. Hebrews 1:11 says all the earthly things will perish. But God will always remain. He will remain the unchangeable God.

5. *a.* What does "unchangeable" mean to you?

b. Why do you think it is important to know that God is unchangeable?

6. Read Luke 21:33.
    a. Besides the eternal God, what else will never pass away?

    b. In your opinion, where is the best place for God's Word to be stored on earth?

    c. How can that be done?

The eternal God! The Alpha and Omega—the beginning and the end. In the modern world of mind-boggling things, the human heart longs for this eternal One and for the peace and assurance He gives. A man who accepted Christ in our church told my husband that he had walked the aisles of the supermarket actually trying to find something that would satisfy the void in him that he couldn't explain.

Christ is from everlasting to everlasting. He is the unchangeable one. He promises eternal life to His children. He keeps His word—and, as they say, "you can take that to the bank!"

Undivided Attention

Read Hebrews 2:1.

1. We are to pay careful attention to what?

Why?

"Pay attention!" Every teacher and parent has said this to a child innumerable times. When we want to say something important to another person, we know we must get his or her attention. The Hebrews writer begins chapter 2 by asking the reader to pay very close attention to what he has said in chapter 1—not just casual attention but very careful attention. Chapter 1 laid out some very important facts about the Son of God, and part of today's verse tells us why we must pay careful attention to them: *so that we do not drift away.* Lowrie gives us this translation: "For this reason we must more abundantly give heed to the things that were heard, lest haply we drift away."[1]

2. Copy a dictionary definition of the word "drift," or write your own.

The Greek word meaning "pay attention" was a nautical word. It referred to taking careful action so that nothing, such as good weather conditions for sailing, could slip by you. It was also used to warn ship captains not to fall asleep and allow their ships to drift and miss the harbor. So the Hebrews writer is very wise to admonish his readers to diligently heed the gospel of Jesus, the Son. Drifting is dangerous.

In the Old Testament the Israelites were given specific instructions for making sure the Scriptures were passed on to their children so they would pay attention to them.

3. Read Deuteronomy 31:9-13.
    a. How often was the complete Law to be read to them?

    b. What are the two reasons given for this action?

Keeping the law before the people was one way of getting them to pay attention. James, who describes himself at the beginning of his letter as a servant of God, writes some very plain words in James 1:22, 25: *Do not merely listen to the word, and so deceive yourselves. Do what it says . . . the man who looks intently into the perfect law that gives freedom, and continues to do this, not forgetting what he has heard, but doing it—he will be blessed in what he does.* Circle the phrase "but doing it."

The New Testament continually stresses the importance of hearing and paying attention to the Word. Hearing, paying attention, and believing are so intertwined.

4. One of the most quoted verses in the New Testament is Romans 10:17. Record it here.

It is important to note in Hebrews 2:1 that we are to pay careful attention to what we have heard. Some teaching in psychology suggests that we have not truly "heard" something until it becomes a part of our life and behavior.

5. *a.* List a few things you believe about God that affect your behavior.

   b. Can you remember when you "heard" them?

6. John 8:47 mentions a very sobering fact. Copy it here.

7. Paying attention to what we hear will include a response. Romans 2:13 says, *It is not those who _____ the _____ who are righteous in God's sight, but it is those who _____ the _____ who will be declared righteous.*

At the close of the parable of the sower in Luke 8, we read these beautiful words: *The seed on good soil stands for those with a noble and good heart, who hear the word, retain it, and by persevering produce a crop* (verse 15). Pay attention!

MEMORY CHALLENGE

He _____ us, not because of _____ things we had _____, but because of his _____.
Titus 3:5

DAY THREE

No Escape!

Read Hebrews 2:2-3.

1. According to Hebrews 2:2, what does each violation and disobedience receive?

Today's scripture contains one of the most serious questions in all of the Bible, and one of the most important: *How shall we escape if we ignore such a great salvation?*

The question is not a "how-to" one. The writer is not asking for instruction on how to escape. He asks the question to stress the fact that there *is* no escape. Escape by any means is unthinkable. Because of His love, God has given us free agency (the power to choose), which also allows us to neglect the message if we so choose. It must be noted, though, that we do not choose the consequences— the consequences have already been decided by God and are taught clearly in His Word.

This question is asked to bring us face to face with what we should already know: God will not be ignored and allow us to escape.

God has given us safeguards. His Word is very important. Violating His Word brings punishment. To be spiritually healthy, we must know His Word.

2. Psalm 119:11 gives a very worthy purpose for studying the Bible. Record it here:

3. Psalm 119 contains many great spiritual goals that all of us should have. Verse 162 says, *I rejoice in your promise like one who finds great spoil.* Psalm 119:167-68 says, *I obey your _____, for I love them greatly. I obey your _____ and your _____, for all my ways are known to you.*

4. Record Psalm 119:174.

5. List four requests the psalmist made in 119:33-36.
   Verse 33—

Verse 34—

Verse 35—

Verse 36—

6. Read 2 Peter 1:3-4. Verse 4 states that Jesus has given His great and precious promises so that through them you may—

    1. _____

    _____

    2. _____

    _____

The question today is—how shall we escape if we *ignore?* In the King James Version of the Bible the word is *neglect. The Living Bible* says *are indifferent to.* They all basically mean the same, but with tiny variations. We could say that to ignore is not to acknowledge; to neglect means to know something is there but not to give it our time or attention; and to be indifferent to something means it doesn't have any significance to us one way or the other, that we could take it or leave it. Scripture cautions us about all three attitudes. When we ignore God, it is not His loss but ours.

7. From Genesis to Revelation the Bible challenges us to be diligent in pursuing God. The following scriptures name some of the precious things we forfeit if we ignore God. List them:

Psalm 29:11 (two)

John 5:24

Romans 5:1

Galatians 5:1

Ephesians 2:18

1 Peter 1:8

Being ignored is very painful, especially when we have truly given of ourselves to something or someone. Sometimes we suffer great sorrow because a person does not respond to our kindness or goodness. Think of what *God* must feel when His Son is ignored and neglected!

Several years ago a missionary nurse, writing about her experiences in Africa, related this story. A native woman appeared at the mission hospital carrying a totally listless, very small baby—a child she had given birth to in that hospital six months before. Angrily, she yelled that she didn't like the baby and would not take care of it. In spite of the nurses' pleadings, she left the baby there and was never seen again.

What a pitiful sight! It was evident that the baby had been neglected; it hardly weighed 10 pounds. A very wise supervisor placed the infant in a crib in the center of the hospital where all four wings of the care center merged. Hospital personnel were instructed to talk to and pat the baby every time they passed the crib. They did! A little pat, words of affection, some singing of lullabies, big smiles. In days the baby's eyes began to focus, color came to her cheeks, and she gradually became aware and alive to her surroundings. She giggled, smiled, and grew. She was no longer neglected!

The Hebrews writer knew that neglect causes death—of relationship, motivation, and life itself. Spiritual life is no exception. The soul of a person will shrink without proper communication with God. And from the consequences of continually neglecting salvation, there is no escape!

MEMORY CHALLENGE

What is *not* the reason He saved us?

Why *did* He save us?

DAY FOUR

A Great Salvation!

Read Hebrews 2:3.

1. Who first announced this great salvation?

2. Record Psalm 96:2.

The death and resurrection of Jesus are the heart of our "great salvation." According to *The World Book Dictionary*, the word "salvation" means (1) a saving or being saved and (2) preservation from destruction, ruin, loss, or calamity. This dictionary also says a "savior" is a person who saves or rescues.[1] The Old testament testifies that being "saved" was always by God. While in the big fish's stomach Jonah said, *Salvation comes from the LORD* (Jonah 2:9). In the New Testament, Matthew 1:21 tells us that the angel told Joseph that the child Mary was carrying would save the people from their sins. And that child, Jesus, gave His life to accomplish that.

3. In writing to the Romans, Paul confirms the fulfillment of the angel's words. Record Romans 5:8.

Usually the value of anything is set by the price we have to pay for it. The harder it is to get, the more it is worth. Not so with the salvation that Jesus provides. When we know Jesus Christ as Savior, the value is not in the price *we* pay for it but the price *He* paid to make salvation free to us. No wonder Hebrews calls it the *great* salvation!

4. The apostle Paul connects the gospel (the Good News) to salvation. Read Romans 1:16 and complete this sentence:

I am not ashamed of the _____, because it is the _____ of _____ for the salvation of everyone who believes.

5. There are so many references in God's Word to this great salvation. Record the ones listed here:

Psalm 27:1

Psalm 62:2

Acts 4:12

2 Corinthians 7:10

Titus 2:11

H. Orton Wiley, a modern theologian, wrote, "This great salvation is the answer to every human problem. It is born out of the majesty of the Son at the right hand of the Father; it is administered in the Church by the Holy Spirit as the gift of the glorified Christ."[2]

Perhaps some of the most important words written by the apostle Paul are recorded in 2 Corinthians 6:1-2. He says we must not receive God's grace in vain. He ends these two verses by saying *Now is the day of salvation*. Paul wrote those words centuries ago, but they are just as important today—maybe more so. *Now* is God's time for us.

MEMORY CHALLENGE

Make a list of things you thank God for, using these letters:

M

E

R

C

Y

God's Own Witness

Read Hebrews 2:4.

1. How did God testify to this great salvation?

As kids we played a game called "Challenge." It was a sort of a "put up or shut up" exercise in boasting. To remain the leader you had to claim you could do something —and then do it. If you couldn't follow through on your claim, the person who successfully called your bluff became the new leader. Of course, believing God's Word and becoming a Christian is no game. But God knows that somewhere in all of us is a skeptical streak. We want to say, "Prove it!" Isn't it wonderful that God has gone to such great lengths to prove He is who He says He is? Today's scripture simply says that God has proven this is a great salvation. He has backed up His claims with signs, wonders, and various miracles.

Sometimes we miss the "signs." And truthfully, His wonders are often wonders to us, too, maybe because we don't look for them! We can't always explain them, because they are not like the ordinary and familiar. But today's verse makes it clear that they are real and come from God himself.

I read of a man who was a new convert and was asked if he believed all the Bible says about miracles. Did he believe that Jesus turned the water into wine? He replied, "Well, in my life He changed booze into food, clothes, and a home for my family!"

2. Sometimes our only ability to explain God is to tell of the miraculous change in our lives. Read John 9:1-11, 25. Record the second part of verse 25:

We should never shy away from claiming God's unusual workings in our life just because we cannot explain them. One of the greatest testimonies we can give is "I just know I'm changed—from point A to point B, from where I was to where I am now in Christ!" or perhaps "I can't explain it. But God has done a great thing in my life!"

Miracles that are of God make an impact on a watching world. John records two occasions when the people believed because of the miracles they saw Jesus perform.

3. *a.* Read John 3:1-2. Who was convinced because of the miracles?

b. Read John 6:5-14. Why did this group of people begin to proclaim Jesus as the Prophet who was to come into the world?

As a child I lived with tremendous fear. I was terribly and unusually afraid of the dark. Even after I was married, I found it a horrible experience to be alone at night. After my husband completed his graduate work for his chosen profession, God called him to preach. That required a different kind of preparation. Because of our living circumstances, it was more reasonable for me to stay in our home and for him to commute to seminary. I was alone four nights each week. I was not just afraid—I was petrified! Each night I sat rigidly, wide-eyed, listening for noises. I perspired. I cried and lost lots of sleep. One night I fell to my knees, cried loudly to God—and He delivered me from my fears. Since that "healing" I have been alone at night more times than I can count, but I have slept like a baby. I have had a peace beyond understanding. This was nothing less than one of God's miracles!

Of course, we cannot read God's mind to know the full intent of signs, wonders, and miracles. But His Word does tell us that they should engender and strengthen our belief.

4. Record John 14:11.

5. Look up John 20:30-31, and complete this passage:

Jesus did many other miraculous signs in the presence of his disciples, which are not recorded in this book. But these are written that you may believe that

_____ _____
_____ _____ ,
_____ _____
_____ _____ ,

and that by believing you may have _____
_____ _____
_____ .

6. The Bible says that God "validated" Jesus by working through Him in various ways. Read Acts 2:22. If you were telling someone about the signs, wonders, and miracles of the Bible, what would your list include?

All these great and wonderful things done by God are not to persuade us to believe. They are to confirm God's omnipotent and sovereign nature. A very interesting scripture is Psalm 119:27, which says, *Let me understand the teaching of your precepts; then I will meditate on your wonders.*

Perhaps it is the little things that add up to a great life. It is the little gestures that speak of the miracle of love; it is the small response of thanks that gives greatness to small deeds, the tiny bits of acceptance that must be present to form a lasting and great bond of friendship. We should make it a way of life to watch for these "little" miracles, the daily wonders and the meaningful signs.

7. Start a record book. For two weeks make note of the miracles and wonders God performs in your daily life. Did He direct you to something you had misplaced? Did He send a word of cheer from a friend exactly when you needed it? Did He protect you from a near-miss accident? Did He give you wisdom for a situation that you didn't know you had? You will see that God's presence and action in your life add up to the *great* signs, wonders, and miracles of God's goodness!!

MEMORY CHALLENGE

Recite this week's verse to someone.

DAY SIX

Testimony of the Holy Spirit

Read Hebrews 2:4.

God is amazing in His consistency! *He gives.* He gave His Son. He gave His Spirit. He gives and gives and gives.

1. How does God distribute the gifts of the Holy Spirit, according to 1 Corinthians 12:7?

God wants the entire human race to know He has provided a great adequate, magnificent salvation. The salvation that Jesus proclaimed He continues to empower and confirm today.

The last phrase of verse 3 says this great salvation *was confirmed to us by those who heard him [the Lord]* —in other words, by way of mouth. Verse 4 states a very important fact: God adds His own testimony by signs, wonders, and miracles; distributing among believers the gifts of the Holy Spirit. These assure us of His involvement with us.

"God is not only a God of the Word, but also a God of power. . . . God is Spirit. . . . The proportion of spiritual power which God imparts to the individual lies within His power. But one thing is certain: where God is at work, there He gives the Word of salvation, the wonder-working power of the Holy Spirit."[1]

2. Reread Hebrews 2:3-4. Who is involved in the following verse?

3—

4 (first part)—

4 (second part)—

Once again the Hebrews writer reminds us of the Godhead: Father, Son, and Holy Spirit. Together they have always been involved in salvation. No wonder it is referred

to as the "great" salvation. And no wonder there is no escape (verse 3) if we neglect this salvation, which is the
work of the Trinity.

3. Verse 4 says there are four ways God testifies to this
    great salvation. What is the fourth one?

    Most of us know someone whose "gift" we admire. It
is important for us to remember that the Holy Spirit gives
the gifts and, in plain words, He decides who gets what!
The truth is that He is greater than His gifts, and He alone
has the wisdom to know what gift fits each of us.

4. Summarize Romans 12:6-8.

5. One of the great challenges to us as Christians is to dis-
    cover and accept the gifts the Spirit has given us per-
    sonally. Record these two important statements:

    1 Corinthians 7:7

    1 Peter 4:10

6. The apostle Paul begins 1 Corinthians 12 with these
    words: *Now about spiritual gifts, brothers, I do not
    want you to be ignorant.* In verses 4-6 he makes it
    clear that God is very involved in the way these gifts
    are used. Fill in the blanks:
    - *There are _____ kinds of _____,
      but the same _____.*
    - *There are _____ kinds of _____,
      but the same _____.*
    - *There are _____ kinds of _____,
      but the same _____ works all of them in all
      men.*

7. Continuing in this same chapter (12), read verses 7-10.
    Record verse 11.

8. The following tasks are optional but can be very help-
    ful:
    a. List three Christian friends who are important to
        you.

        What gifts do you feel they have?

    b. What gifts do you feel you have?

    c. For the brave: ask a cherished friend or family mem-
        ber what he or she sees as your gift or gifts.

    d. With answers to *b* and *c* before you, ask God to show
        you how you can best use your gifts.

    Today's scripture from Hebrews states that the gifts
the Holy Spirit gives testify of "a great salvation" for those
who follow Christ. It should be a privilege to nurture and
develop them; to let the Holy Spirit use them for the "common good" of His children. In the parable of the talents
found in Matthew 25:14-18, we find a very important lesson: it is not how much we have been given but how we
use our gifts that counts. We dare not waste them. By the
help of the Holy Spirit we will not!
    "Between the great things we cannot do and the small
things we will not do, the danger is that we shall do nothing."[2]

MEMORY CHALLENGE

Say this week's verse to God, and add *Thank You*.

Hebrews

LESSON 4

■ A Study of Hebrews 2

DAY ONE

Oh, How He Cares!

Read Hebrews 2, concentrating on verses 5-9.

1. Fill in the words from Hebrews 2:6:

   *What is _____ that you are _____ of him,
   the _____ of _____ that you _____ for
   _____?*

   Think of it! He is mindful of us and cares for us. These two questions in verse 6 are quoted often, particularly by preachers and evangelists, to emphasize the insignificance of humanity as compared to the magnificence of the Son of God, the God whom the Hebrews writer has been talking about. The "wonder" they express is centuries old, for verses 6-8 are a direct quotation from the words of David in Psalm 8:4-6.

   Isn't it amazing (almost mind-boggling) that Almighty God (Father, Son, and Holy Spirit) should pay attention to mere human beings? The following two quotes are humorous but really do describe us:
   - "Man is akin to clod and cherubim!" (Francis Thompson).
   - "[We are] as the glory and scum of the universe!" (Blaise Pascal).[1]

2. Record Job 7:17.

3. There is only one kind of motivation that could prompt anyone, especially God, to be mindful of human beings—it is divine love. Record 1 John 3:1.

4. Complete this wonderful truth found in 1 Peter 1:18-19:

   *You know that it was not with _____ things
   such as _____ or _____ that you were
   _____ from the _____ way of life
   handed down to you from your forefathers, but with
   the _____ _____ of _____, a
   _____ without _____ or _____.*

5. Read Romans 8:3.

   a. In whose likeness did God's Son appear?

   b. For what reason?

When God sent His Son, He did not send a giant, a powerful magician, a likeness of a huge statue blazing with fire or lights of glory. He honored His greatest creation by sending Jesus in our likeness. He came as one of us!

Hebrews 2:6-8 needs a little clarification. The phrase "son of man" is referring to humanity. In the Book of Ezekiel, God addresses Ezekiel over 80 times as "son of man." But human beings in God's order are not lower than the angels, nor is Jesus. Most commentators agree that the actual wording of the Greek text in verse 7 is "you made him, *for a little while,* lower than the angels," referring to humanity. This also applies to verse 9. It should read, "Jesus, who **for a little while** . . . was made a little lower than the angels."

Even though Hebrews refers to Jesus many times from 1:1 through 2:8, the name "Jesus" is not used until verse 9. And then the writer says, *We see Jesus.* To see Jesus should be our constant desire.

There are several very important truths about our salvation in verse 9. Jesus suffered death. He was crowned with glory and honor that all persons might be saved. It was all because of the grace of God—not because of the wrath of God, or because Jesus should have power to make us suffer, but because of His grace, which is goodness, love, and gentleness. He came to make it possible for us to be what we ought to be!

6. Record 2 Thessalonians 2:16-17.

Commentator William Barclay says that verses 5-9 tell us three things: (1) the ideal of what we should be, (2) what we actually are, and (3) what we can become. Prayerfully ask God to show you where you are in this process. Make some notes to help you to know how to pray this week. Remember how much He cares for you, and that wherever you are, that is where He is. He loves you and reigns *over all!*

Perfection of Suffering

Read Hebrews 2:9-10.

1. *a.* Why was Jesus crowned with glory and honor? (See verse 9.)

b. What was the reason for His death? (See verse 9.)

Jesus was called *a man of sorrows*, but He was also a man of joy. His joy came in the midst of and because of His suffering.

2. Read Nehemiah 8:9-10. Ezra the priest had been reading the Book of the Law to the people. Record the last sentence of verse 10.

God's people have always desired the *joy of the Lord.* But H. C. G. Moule reminds us that "Joy is shallow that is not rooted in the soil of suffering."[1] The birth of a child is an example of his statement. The pain of the suffering brings forth the joy of the birth.

One of the greatest challenges for us is to somehow understand the mind of God. Of course, that is impossible to do completely. However, God opens little windows of insights for us from His Word. So as we seek to know God, perhaps our first assignment as Christians is to diligently read His Word. Because we, too, are destined to suffer from time to time, we must be aware that His Word is our very life!

3. Jesus knew He was to suffer. In Luke 24 we read the account of Jesus walking with two of His followers on the road to Emmaus following His resurrection. They did not recognize Him and told Him about the Crucifixion and Resurrection. Record the words of Jesus in verse 26.

4. Read Mark 8:31-33. Peter's reaction when Jesus predicted His death was very understandable: he did not want Jesus to suffer; after all, He was the Christ. Jesus rebuked Peter. Record His words in verse 33.

These words should challenge us to know Jesus and His words better and better. It is by this process that we move (although sometimes slowly) from "the things of men" to "the things of God."

5. By the time Peter wrote his letters, he had come to understand the dynamics of suffering. Read 1 Peter 4:12-16. This passage contains many important thoughts. Fill in the missing words:

13: *But _____ that you _____ in the _____ of Christ . . .*

14: *If you are _____ because of the _____ of _____, you are _____, for the _____ of _____ and of God _____ on you.*

16: *If you _____ as a _____, do not be _____, but _____ _____ that you _____ that _____.*

The desire of the Christian's heart is to know Christ, to mature in the Christian experience, and to become more like Him. God desires for us to grow spiritually, and one of the ways to do this is shown as the path of suffering. 1 Peter 2:21 testifies to this by saying, *To this you were called, because Christ suffered for you, leaving you an example, that you should follow in his steps.* Though we may not cherish the thought, following His steps will lead us through suffering and sorrow.

We might ask, "How dare God allow the enemy access to this sacred bond between the Savior and the saved?" Wait a minute. Christians need not for one minute be upset or sidetracked because the enemy is alive and well and may attack or tempt us. We should rejoice not only that God has such great confidence in His power to sustain us but also that the born-again person has the ability to withstand the worst the enemy has to throw at him or her. God promises the strength, and He trusts us! Isn't that exciting?

T. W. Willingham wrote, "If one can but see that life's tests are gateways to perfection, he can begin to understand why Peter could say, 'But rejoice,' and James enjoin, 'Count it all joy.' One may learn to be happy in the process, for the process procures peace."[2]

Before a trip I made to China, I contacted P. K. and Mary Li, asking permission to visit them while I was in Shanghai. They graciously said yes. This couple were vital influences in the establishment of our denomination in China before World War II. In that war their persecution was extensive—during the war because they were American-born, and following Mao Tse Tung's revolution be-cause they were of "the intellect." To Mao, "the intellect" was the real enemy.

Dr. Li was one of the most brilliant medical doctors China has ever known. His persecution required him to scrub the floors of the very hospital where he had practiced and taught medicine. Mrs. Li, who had a doctorate in literature, spent many years under house arrest. Imagine not being allowed to leave your tiny home for years! I will never forget my entrance into their home. I felt I was entering a palace and was so humbled. The presence of God was so real and triumphant in that place. I have never viewed myself as a visionary, but I say without apology that everywhere, on the simple, bare furniture, on everything on the walls, and on their glowing 80-some-year-old faces I saw victory. These were two of the most radiant Christians I have ever met. Here indeed was triumph!

6. Record Paul's words in Romans 8:18.

7. Do you feel you are presently suffering in some way? Trust God with His plan for you. Write a prayer asking Him to bring glory out of your suffering.

MEMORY CHALLENGE

What kind of Shepherd is Jesus?

What does He do for His sheep?

DAY THREE

The Family of God

Read Hebrews 2:11-13.

Complete verse 11:

*Both _____ _____ who makes _____
_____ and those who are _____ _____ are
of the _____ _____.*

Today's verse describes the standard for being a member of God's family: holiness. We are to be holy people. It is interesting that the Bible often refers to Jesus as *from* the Father, and us, His creation, as *of* the Father. That is probably because God *makes* us what we are spiritually. We become spiritual children by the divine inbreathing of the Holy Spirit of God. This experience puts us spiritually in the same family with Jesus Christ. Isn't that exciting?

There are three distinct divisions in today's Scripture verses.

1. God (the one who makes us holy) is holy.

a. Record 1 Peter 1:15-16, and underline the last four words.

b. Everything about God is holy.
Psalm 20:6 says His _____ is holy.
Psalm 47:8 says His _____ is holy.
Psalm 97:12 says His _____ is holy.

c. Revelation 4 records one of the most sacred scenes in the Bible. It is the description of God's throne in heaven, where the creatures before the throne never stop praising the Almighty. Record their words at the end of verse 8:

2. God's children are holy.
The Bible teaches that we must repent, confess our sins, and confess Jesus as Lord. Following that, the Bible says, we are to *offer [our] bodies as living sacrifices, holy and pleasing to God* (Romans 12:1). Even though there are those who question how people can be holy, the Bible says plainly that it is possible through God and the Holy Spirit. In fact, as we have read, 1 Peter 1:15-16 says *be holy in all you do*, and *be holy*, which is a commandment.

a. Read Ephesians 4:22-24. Record verse 24.

b. Read Ephesians 5:1. We are to be _____ of _____.

c. Read 1 Thessalonians 4:7. God calls us to do what?

d. In Ephesians 4:25-32 we read a list of things expected of Christians. Summarize what each of these say:
29—

30—

31—

32—

These expectations are a part of living holy before God: having a right relationship with Him and with our fellow human beings. When we live as God prescribes, we can understand what Hebrews says in today's verse: *Jesus is not ashamed to call [us] brothers.*

3. We are family!
One of the great descriptions the Bible gives of Jesus and the redeemed is God's calling us family. We were once outcasts, but now we are "kin."
"So great is His sanctifying power through the Holy Spirit, and so great the spiritual restoration of the sanctified, that He is no longer ashamed to call us brethren."[1]
"Family" stirs our memories and emotions. Some may be negative ones. Two statements are needed here: (1) Not all persons come from a "happy" family background, and (2) the "family" is much different than it once was. Just today one of the headlines in the daily newspaper read, "TV Shows Reflect Demise of Traditional Family Life." It reminds me of a famous line spoken by Dorothy in *The Wizard of Oz:* "I don't think we're in Kansas anymore!"
There is no doubt things have changed in the world in which we live. But being a member of the family of God means that even with our differences, if we are "born again," we are in the family of God. We are very

different, but we are *one*. And we must live by the rules of God's Word. My father, who was a gentle man, had basically one rule for our household: "As long as you live in my house, you will live by its rules!" Maybe he got that idea from God!

a. Record Hebrews 12:14:

Make _____ effort to live in _____.

b. First Peter 3:8 says,

Finally, all of you, live in harmony with one another;

be _____,

love as _____,

be _____ and _____.

MEMORY CHALLENGE

Write the memory verse on a Post-it note or 3" x 5" card and attach it somewhere that's easily noticed.

DAY FOUR

Victory over Satan!

Read Hebrews 2:14-16.

1. What did Jesus share with His children?

Today's verses tell in a nutshell why Jesus came to earth to live, die, and be resurrected. He did it all to bring about our salvation. How better to identify with humanity? I don't ever want to appear disrespectful, but it is a comfort to know that when it comes to life and death, Jesus can say, "Been there, done that!"

2. Record the last part of verse 14, beginning with *so that.*

Jesus came not to destroy death itself but to destroy the *power* of death: the devil. We certainly do not like the truth that we must fight Satan, the enemy. Nevertheless, this is a reality recorded from Genesis to Revelation. We hardly get past *In the beginning* in Genesis 1:1 until we read that not all is well in paradise—there is an enemy. And the righteous must fight him in God's strength.

This battle is between a *loving* God and a *lying* enemy. The enemy is active, deadly, and untrustworthy. Jesus said some very strong things to a group of argumentative Jews about this enemy.

3. Read John 8:44, and fill in the words of this portion:

You _____ to your _____, the devil, and you want to carry out your _____ _____.
He was a _____ from the beginning, not holding to the _____, for there is no _____ in him.

4. Read these verses: Ephesians 1:3; 2:6; 3:10. What two-word phrase is found in each of these?

Read Ephesians 6:12. Who is also found in the heavenly realms?

Can you believe that? Satan in the heavenly realms? We must understand that Paul is referring to the heavenly realms as the "elevated" conditions the born-again people enjoy here on earth. The blessings (Ephesians 1:3) and the position (Ephesians 2:6) are ours while on earth. It is in these areas in our lives while we are on earth that Satan *holds the power of death,* as Hebrews 2:14 says.

Today's verses (Hebrews 2:14-16) record some of the greatest news ever written. We can be conquerors because Christ came to defeat Satan.

5. Read 1 Peter 4:12-16, and write three phrases that you like:

_____

_____

_____

6. We must be "armed" to fight the enemy. Ephesians 6:13-17 gives us some instructions for being prepared. We should put on—

   the _____ _____ _____,
   to hold the armor in place;

   the _____ _____ _____,
   to protect the heart;

   the _____, to prepare the feet for activity;

   the _____ _____ _____,
   to intercept the enemy's missiles;

   the _____ _____ _____,
   to help us keep our head;

   the _____ _____ _____
   _____, the Word, our defense!

After a loud yet wondrous time of prayer in our church, one dear member of our congregation loved to say even louder, "Well, praise the Lord! It's none of the devil's business!" Since everyone within a block heard him, I'm sure the devil did too!

Satan does have "business." His business is to bring spiritual death to us all. But Jesus came to earth and died to destroy any power over us that Satan may have. If you struggle with a particular attitude or situation that hinders your spiritual exuberance, pledge today to pray about it every time it comes to mind. Stay with it—Jesus will set you free!

MEMORY CHALLENGE

Write the memory verse in this space:

DAY FIVE

Free Indeed!

Read Hebrews 2:14-17.

1. Verse 15 gives a second reason Jesus died. What was that reason?

Ancient civilizations had long lists of ways to find favor with the gods. These were supposed to assure a "glorious" something after death. When the writer of Hebrews wrote this letter, the peoples of the earth were "slaves" emotionally and intellectually to the fear of death. One of Satan's works was to control people by the fear of death and eternal damnation. And this fear was based in slavery to sin, from which, supposedly, there was no deliverance possible.

2. But through Jesus was a better way. The apostle Paul knew about deliverance. Read Romans 6:15-18, and complete these words of verses 17-18:

   But _____ be to _____ that, though you used to be _____ to _____, you wholeheartedly obeyed the form of teaching to which you were entrusted. You have been _____ _____ from _____ and have become _____ to _____.

It was not just inevitable that Christ should die—it was necessary. It was by His death that He delivered all of us from the devil's power to destroy us simply by using the fear of death.

"Because Christ's death was followed by His resurrection, He showed that death does not have the final word in human existence. He destroyed him that had the power of death, that is, the devil."[1]

The World Book Dictionary defines the word "slave" in these two ways:
   1. a person who is the property of another;
   2. a person who submits to or follows another.[2]

It is our responsibility to guard our thinking and actions with diligence. My minister husband said many times, "Whatever gets your attention gets *you!*"

3. Record the last part of 2 Peter 2:19.

4. This problem is stated clearly in Romans 7:24-25. Verse 24 states the problem: *What a wretched man I am! Who will rescue me from this body of death?* Record the answer as stated in verse 25.

Death is not the only enemy to be feared. Sin will enslave those who will allow Satan to tempt and lure them into a "comfort" zone regarding sin. There is nothing so sad or frightening as those who are slaves to sin and its allure.

5. Jesus spoke a very serous truth in John 8:34. He said, *I tell you the truth, everyone who sins is a slave to sin.* Read verses 35-36, and record verse 36.

It is absolutely necessary as Christians to examine our priorities from time to time. Good habits are developed by constant diligence. If you are in bondage to any negative habit or attitude, God can set you free. And He wants to. He delights in breaking the chains that bind us!

These are the words of Jesus from John 8:31-32: *If you hold to my teaching, you are really my disciples. Then you will know the truth, and the truth will set you free* (emphasis added).

6. Read the preceding verse (John 8:32) slowly, and personalize it by using your name in place of the underlined words. Ask God to examine your life: actions, thoughts, and motives. Let Him reveal to you any areas of your life that need to be adjusted. Then read the following scripture aloud: *It is for freedom that Christ has set us free. Stand firm, then, and do not let yourselves be burdened again by a yoke of slavery* (Galatians 5:1).

MEMORY CHALLENGE

Sometime today meditate on the Good Shepherd. Recite the memory verse to end your meditation.

DAY SIX

Help with Temptation

Read Hebrews 2:18.

1. Jesus was tempted while on earth. What is the result of His being tempted?

All of us will be tempted but not necessarily in identical circumstances. Temptations will not all be similar in nature, because they come to people of different backgrounds, lifestyles, ages, and dispositions. Having said that, we should note that Satan tempts us with one or two purposes in mind: to get us to deny Jesus, or to persuade us to disobey what we know is His will. Taking either road leads us to spiritual compromise and destruction.

2. *a.* Read James 1:2-4. Starting with 3, complete his words: *because you know that the _____ of your _____ develops _____. Perseverance must _____ its work so that you may be _____ and _____, not _____ anything.*

   b. Read Matthew 26:41. What two things should we do to avoid temptation?

Since the Scriptures state that God *tested* some individuals, a distinction must be made between a "test" and a "temptation." God allows the testing of our faith that we might discover our ability to withstand. He then helps us with any lack of spiritual stamina. On the other hand, a temptation is Satan's way of trying to provoke, lure, or entice us to do something that we know is against God's law and will. A very good evaluation of our problem is to remember that God *tests* us to make us stand; Satan *tempts* us to make us stumble.

3. A record of the temptation of Jesus is found in Matthew 4:1-11.

   a. The first temptation (verses 1-4) deals with Jesus' physical need. Why could Jesus have been tempted to change the stones to bread?

b. Temptation 2 is recorded in verses 5-7. Satan recognized the power Jesus had to control the natural forces of the earth. Here he appealed to Jesus to defy the laws of nature, saying that He would not be hurt physically by such a jump. What could Jesus have "gained" from such an unheard-of feat?

c. The last temptation was to set up a kingdom for Jesus, but one that would come into being by force. Read Luke 17:20-21, and record the last eight words.

4. Complete the words of Jesus in John 18:36.

My _____ is not of this _____. If it were, my _____ would _____ to prevent my arrest by the Jews. But now my _____ is from another place.

5. a. In general terms, how are all of us tempted?

b. Describe a circumstance in which temptation to disobey God's Word would be very great.

Jesus had dedicated himself to the way of the Cross. In His temptations Satan offered Him a way to carry out His ministry by bypassing the Cross. Many times our temptations are routes to immediate success or gratification. They are supposed shortcuts to spiritual maturity. Satan often claims great results, but we must learn that compromise is never God's plan. I have known many wonderful people who have given in to temptation only to find they could not handle the consequences.

6. The progression of temptation is stated so clearly in James 1:13-15. Fill in the blanks:

For _____ cannot be _____ by _____, nor does he _____ anyone; but each one is _____ when, by his own _____ _____, he is _____ away and _____.

Then, after _____ has _____, it gives _____ to _____; and _____, when it is _____ gives _____ to _____.

God's Word is so wonderful to provide just the strength and promise we need. The following scriptures are very special:

- 1 Corinthians 10:13-14—*No temptation has seized you except what is common to man. And God is faithful; he will not let you be tempted beyond what you can bear. But when you are tempted, he will also provide a way out so that you can stand up under it.*
- James 1:12—*Blessed is the man who perseveres under trial, because when he has stood the test, he will receive the crown of life that God has promised to those who love him.*

One of the best promises is today's scripture: *Because he himself suffered when he was tempted, he is able to help those who are being tempted* (Hebrews 2:18).

Mrs. Charles Cowman in *Streams in the Desert* tells this story: A dear old saint was asked what she would do if a fierce temptation overtook her. Her quick reply was "I would lift up my hands to the Lord and say, 'Lord, your property is in danger. Take care of it quick!' Then I'd forget about it 'till I was tried again.'"[1] Sounds good to me!

MEMORY CHALLENGE

Repeat the memory verse by at least three different times of the day.

Hebrews

LESSON 5

■ A study of Hebrews 3

DAY ONE

Noble Thoughts!

Read Hebrews 3, concentrating on verse 1.

1. On whom should we fix our thoughts?

   What two titles are given to Jesus?

The beginning word of Hebrews 3 is *Therefore*. It connects chapters 1 and 2 with chapter 3. Having established the identify of Jesus as sovereign, holy, and above all others, the writer begins instructions for developing as a child of God. Since Jesus is holy and one with the Father, the Body of Christ must pay attention to its conduct and display the results of that relationship.

Today's scripture contains two very important words: "fix" and "thoughts." The Greek word for "fix" is not used often in the New Testament. In the Old Testament the same idea is often translated from the Hebrew language as "steadfast."

2. Record Deuteronomy 11:18.

3. Read Psalm 57:7. What is steadfast?

   Read the verse again, substituting "fixed" for "steadfast."

4. Psalm 112 is a description of a righteous person who fears the Lord and delights in His commands. Record verse 7.

In the New Testament Jesus used the word translated "fix" at least twice. Keep in mind that this word is a very strong command for determined action. In Greek it means to concentrate on or gaze at something so intently that what you are seeing becomes a part of you.

5. Read Luke 16:19-26. Jesus is teaching His disciples some very important truths. Summarize verse 26, remembering that the word "fixed" is a permanent condition.

Read Luke 12:24. "The word ["consider"] means to fix the attention on something in such a way that the inner meaning of the thing, the lesson that the thing is designed to teach, may be learned. In Luke 12:24 Jesus uses the same word when He says: *'Consider the ravens.'* He does not merely mean, 'Look at the ravens.' He means, 'Look at the ravens and understand and learn the lesson that God is seeking to teach you through them.'"[1]

MEMORY CHALLENGE

Hebrews 3:6

And we are his house, ~~house~~ Temple if we hold on to our courage and the hope of which we boast.

We may conclude, then, that the Christian is one whose loyalty to Jesus is fixed. It is very important to be "stubborn" about the nature and focus of our thoughts. *On purpose* we focus our thoughts on Jesus.

Most people would not readily expose all their thoughts to their friends. For one thing, we aren't sure whom we can trust. Not so with Jesus—He can absolutely be trusted!

6. Record the following verses:

Psalm 94:11

Psalm 139:23

Experts in the study of the mind say that every thought that has ever crossed our mind is stored there and can be brought to the surface any time by various things: a word, a scent, a scene. Saturating our minds with thoughts of God and His Word is one of the greatest things we can do for ourselves. Jesus wants our full attention. He deserves it. This concentration should be the basis of every activity of our lives.

Fixing our thoughts on Jesus calls us to a kind of worship. It is devotional. We are constantly called *by* God *to* God.

An old man was asked if it were possible to keep bad thoughts out of his head. "Probably not," he said. "I may not be able to keep a vulture from landing in my tree, but I can sure keep him from building a nest there."

> *Thus ever on through life we find*
> *To trust, O Lord, is best.*
> *Who serve Thee with a quiet mind*
> *Find in Thy service rest.*
> *Their outward troubles may not cease,*
> *But this their joy will be—*
> *"Thou wilt keep him in perfect peace*
> *Whose mind is stayed on Thee."*
> —Author unknown

DAY TWO

The House of God

Read Hebrews 3:6.

1. Record the first sentence of Hebrews 3:6.

The Scriptures constantly admonish us to strive for personal qualities that make us true witnesses to the strength of God in our lives.

2. *a.* Record the second sentence of Hebrews 3:6.

    b. Underline the two qualities listed.

3. God has a house. Summarize what the following scriptures say about that house:

Matthew 12:25

2 Corinthians 5:1

Galatians 6:10

In today's scripture the Hebrews writer stresses that our status as residents of God's house must include two essential qualities.

4. Read 1 Corinthians 16:13-14. What five instructions are given in this verse by the apostle Paul?

    1.

    2.

3.

4.

5.

Courage has always been an admirable quality. *The World Book Dictionary* defines the word as "fearlessness in the face of danger."[1] In the Bible we read meaningful examples of this. Time after time a biblical person displayed courage.

5. *a.* Read Deuteronomy 31:6-8. Moses is speaking to the children of Israel to prepare them for crossing the Red Sea. Name two qualities he instructed them to have (verse 7).

   1.

   2.

   b. Record verse 8.

   c. 2 Chronicles 32:7-8 tells how King Sennacherib of Assyria invaded Judah. When Hezekiah, God's man, addressed the people of Judah, he encouraged them to be _____ and _____ (verse 7).

   d. Hezekiah continued with a very important fact. Record the first sentence of verse 8:

6. Along with courage, today's verse says we must cling to hope. Record Psalm 62:5.

Today's psychologists state that one of the most devastating and dangerous conditions for a human being is to feel that he or she is without hope. It is imperative that the individual have even a small grain of hope. Without it,

every adversity and setback is potentially very dangerous. In the Christian, hope resides in the heart, placed there and nourished by God himself. And this hope engenders other wonderful assets.

7. *a.* What goes hand-in-hand with hope in the following two scriptures?

   Romans 8:25

   Romans 12:12

   b. How does Hebrews 6:19 describe hope?

H. Orton Wiley wrote, "If therefore we would know the faithfulness of Christ and the joy of His fellowship, we must surrender to Him the keys of our lives. He must be the abiding Presence within our hearts; and this, not as a Guest, but as Host. We are His house, and He must have access to every room, and the management and control of all must be in His hands. The test of genuine consecration is the keeping of the keys in His hands, not only during the periods of success and joy, but also in the times of sorrow and adversity."[2]

Prayerfully ask God to examine your spiritual "house." Is He welcome in every room? Is He Lord over all your activities? Does He control all your actions and your thinking? Only you and the Lord know the answers to these questions—but together you have the power to make it so!

MEMORY CHALLENGE

Write this week's memory verse on a Post-it note, and attach it to the refrigerator. Read it each time you open the door.

The Heart of the Matter!

Read Hebrews 3:7-12.

1. Read the entire six verses of today's scripture carefully.

   a. Record verse 12:

   Perhaps this is one of the most serious verses in the Bible itself. Certainly it is important to the Book of Hebrews. It is a great admonition, because it refers to two conditions of the heart unacceptable to God.

   b. They are _____ and _____.

   Every bad disposition, selfish motive, and evil deed finds its root in the sinful and/or unbelieving heart. Let us examine three truths relative to this verse.

■ **The sinful heart**

   The background verses (Hebrews 3:7-11) are quotations from several Old Testament passages, in particular Psalm 95:7-11. The message is an appeal for the Hebrews to listen to the voice of God. Verses 7-8 warn against "hardening" the heart in rebellion—a very dangerous condition. Together these three adjectives ("hardened," "sinful," and "unbelieving") describe a tragic, disastrous condition and life.

2. Record 1 John 3:4.

   The World Book Dictionary defines "lawless" as "uncontrolled and ungovernable."[1] That would help explain God's strong condemnation of it. God must govern our hearts in order to be God to us.

3. The heart (inner being) can harbor a great range of sinful attitudes. List the ones referred to in the following scriptures:

   Leviticus 19:17

   Psalm 28:3

   Jeremiah 5:23

   Matthew 5:28

Romans 1:24

   The children of Israel constantly wavered between the great goodness and deliverance of Jehovah God and their own tendency toward sin and unbelief. Because of their disobedient hearts, they wandered years in the wilderness.

■ **The unbelieving heart**

   To "disbelieve" means the mind and heart have gone through a process concerning what the ear has heard and what the inner self has been confronted with—and then rejects the truth. To refuse to examine and believe God's Word is precarious.

4. Jesus spoke very strong words about rejecting His words. Record John 12:48.

5. Read Revelation 21:8. Unbelievers are linked with a despicable group of eight types of people. List the other seven in this verse.

■ **The heart of a person determines his or her actions.**

   Belief in God must become a life-changing force. A heart yielded to God will develop into a pleasing example of His love and grace.

6. *a.* Read 1 Chronicles 28:9. What two things does God do?

   b. Read Psalm 44:20-21. What does God know?

7. The Psalms are favorites of many people because they echo what we feel, want, and need so much. Read Psalm 119:10-16. Record verses 11 and 16 as a paragraph. Ask God to remind you of this resolve often.

Fill in the blanks:
And we are _____ _____, if we _____ on to our _____ and the _____ of which we boast.

Hebrews 3:6

Encouragement

Read Hebrews 3:13.

Today's scripture assigns to us a very important task: encouraging others—daily. That implies that there is never a day when no one needs encouragement. It also indicates that our involvement with others is to be a vital part of our activity as children of God. Since some translations capitalize the word "Today," it can be thought that it has been set apart from its normal meaning. And in a sense it has, for in the Greek it means "while life lasts," as long as we breathe.

1. *a.* Read Joshua 1:1-9. Joshua has succeeded Moses and must lead the Israelites across the Jordan River. God speaks to him.

   b. Record the last sentence of verse 5.

   c. In verses 6, 7, and 9, the Lord repeats a very important instruction. What is it?

   d. In Joshua 1:1-9 find at least three other directives:
      7—

      8—

      9—

2. Record Proverbs 30:5.

The Old Testament story of David has many inspirational incidents, especially David's friendship with Jonathan (Saul's son), which is a great example of the power of encouragement. King Saul, Jonathan's father, pursues David because he has been designated by God to succeed Saul. Saul had determined to dispose of David by any means available, and his jealously fills David with fear.

3. Read 1 Samuel 23:15-16. What great thing does Jonathan do for David?

4. Words of encouragement aren't just for the moment. Remembrance often brings help and comfort to us when the one who spoke them to us is not even around. Jonathan's words helped David on another occasion. Read 1 Samuel 30:6. Record the last sentence.

God is the great encourager, and His Word is the best encouragement we can offer others. Sometimes we shy away from the role of encourager because we aren't sure exactly what to say. Quoting God's Word or directing someone to His Word is *always* sure and profitable.

5. The following scriptures can be helpful tools for all of us. You need not have them all memorized—just at hand. Write an important thought from each of the following scriptures.
   1 Kings 8:56—

   Romans 4:21 (Paul is referring to Abraham)—

   1 Corinthians 10:13—

6. Read 1 Peter 5:10. What will God do for us after we suffer for a little while?

William Barclay's translation of Hebrews 3:13 reads, "But keep on exhorting each other day by day, so long as the term 'today' can be used, lest any among you be hardened in heart by the seductiveness of sin."[1]

The implication is a serious one—that without fellowship and encouragement from others, there are those who may give up and yield to the temptation of sin. To be an encourager, one does not have to be a "seasoned" Christian. Neither does one have to be versed in psychology or theology or any other "ology." We have only to be available! God will use us beyond our own expectations and abilities if we but proclaim our availability to Him with the sincere prayer *Use me.* Dare to pray those words, and He will!

How do we know we are His house?

Keeping Confidence

Read Hebrews 3:14.

1. Record Hebrews 3:14.

The King James Version of the Bible in Hebrews 3:14 uses the phrase *partakers with Christ.* Some translations use the word "partners," "sharers," or "companions." According to Wiley, to the Hebrew the implication was that "as ancient Israel in the journey to the promised land were the companions of Moses, so in the spiritual journey of life we are to become companions of Christ." Wiley goes on to say, "This is a precious thought that our salvation consists in the possession of Christ himself. He is our Way, our Truth, and our Life."[1]

All of us encounter many people in our lifetime. Some are passing acquaintances, some occasional friends, but some are "companions"! We share common likes, dislikes, interests, ideas, and offer comfort, fellowship, and support to each other. As Christ's followers, we must not be merely acquaintances or occasional worshipers. We are to consult Him or proclaim Him "Lord" not only in isolated times of emergency, need, or sorrow. We are to share *in* Him at all times.

2. Record 1 John 1:7.

Fellowship with one another refers to the activity between the believer and God. Our fellowship with Him is contingent on our constant walk and talk with Him. Our confidence must always be in Christ. The Greek word for "confidence" also means openness, boldness, and a sense of freedom.

"The Greek word 'parresia' indicates a condition that comes from a relationship with God. It also indicates a bold view of the future. We look ahead with confidence because we know that Jesus is in control."[2]

3. Record Hebrews 3:6 and Hebrews 3:14 as one paragraph.

4. Read Philippians 3:3. Here Paul names three qualities of the Christian that will help keep his or her relationship an ongoing, lasting one. List them.

The Scriptures provide many references to the confidence we can have in Christ. Proverbs 3:26 says, *The LORD will be your confidence and will keep your foot from being snared.* Philippians 1:6 says, *being confident of this, that he who began a good work in you will carry it on to completion until the day of Christ Jesus.*

5. *a.* Record 1 John 3:21.

   b. Read 1 John 3:22.

   If we have the confidence of verse 21, we may receive what we ask of Him. What two conditions must we meet in order to claim this promise?

There is no doubt that our confidence must be strong. It must endure not just in prosperity or good times—it must be steady even if and when our world falls apart.

6. Habakkuk was a prophet who endured great suffering. But throughout it all, he kept the confidence that God was supreme and in control. Read his beautiful proclamation in Habakkuk 3:17-18. Record verse 19.

7. Read Psalm 27:3. Write this verse in your own words as if you were writing to tell a friend how solid your determination and confidence in the Lord is.

"The God who holds the sea in the hollow of His hand, who swings this ponderous earth in its orbit, who marshals stars and guides planets, is this very God who says, 'If ye ask, I will do!'"[3]

Recite the verse to a friend or family member. Ask him or her to choose two key words.

The Other Side of the Coin

Read Hebrews 3:16-19.

Although we are not certain who wrote the Book of Hebrews, we can be sure the author was very knowledgeable about the Old Testament Israelites and their relationship to God. God had revealed himself to them in many ways. He had charted their path and given them specific instructions and directions.

1. Drawing from their history, the Hebrews writer reminded the Jews of the New Testament of three conditions unacceptable to God. List them:

   Verse 17

   Verse 18

   Verse 19

   This is a somber passage of Scripture. Both Old and New Testaments confirm in various ways the great danger of disobeying God and also His intolerance of unbelief. The wrath of God is very serious.

2. The Old Testament Book of Numbers records for us a glimpse into God's wrath.

   a. Read Numbers 14:21-24. God refers to the good land promised to all of them. Record verse 23.

   What qualified Caleb to be the exception?

   b. We do not "reap" alone. Read Numbers 14:33-36. Who else paid a great price for the unbelief of the adult Israelites?

   In His Word God teaches how dangerous disbelief is. He is not an unreasonable God. His Word tells of His love for us and offers a great store of knowledge to us about Him. It tells of His nature. It tells us how to become one of His redeemed children. It tells what He can and will do for us. Unbelief is like a slap in the face of a holy, omnipotent God.

3. *a.* Read John 10:22-28. Record verse 25.

   b. In verse 27, what two things does Jesus say His sheep do?

4. Read Genesis 3:1-6. What did the serpent (Satan) convince Eve of?

5. The Gospel of John contains many revelations concerning the consequences of disbelief. Many of us know John 3:16 from memory. If you do not, read it again. Then read John 3:17-18, and record verse 18.

6. According to John 12:48, what two things will bring God's judgment?

   Because the second coming of Christ has not happened after all these centuries, many people scoff at the belief that Jesus will come back to earth. Peter writes plainly about this time to come.

7. Read 2 Peter 3:1-8. What does verse 8 say we must not forget?

8. *a.* Read Revelation 21:6-8. Record verse 7.

We must not forget that there is the "other side of the coin." "Unbelieving" is listed with several horrible sins.

   b. What will happen to this group, according to verse 8?

   All of us are enriched and sustained by the wonderful store of good things given and promised in God's Word to His born-again children. We love the positives. We love the thought of peace, love, victory, and eternal bliss. But God's Word also teaches His wrath, subsequent punishment, and eternal separation from Him. The one thing He will not do is make our choice for us. We must believe or not believe; we cannot pick and choose from His Word whatever suits our fancy.

   I am closing this lesson by praying at this moment that God will search my heart and see if there is any unbelief in me, or if I doubt any part of His Word. If so, I am giving my questions and unbelief to Him unreservedly. Won't you join me?

MEMORY CHALLENGE

Recite the memory verse, and ask God to help you have the two qualities it mentions.

Hebrews

LESSON 6

■ A study of Hebrews 4

DAY ONE

Belief at Its Best

Read Hebrews 4:1-16, concentrating on verses 1-2.

1. Record Hebrews 4:2.

I remember hearing as a child about a minister who often said, "Stand in front of a group of people and yell, 'Fire!' You'll know immediately those who believe you. They'll *act*."

The background scripture to today's verses is Numbers 14:12-23. In a nutshell, the children of Israel, even though they professed faith in God, refused to claim and inhabit Canaan, the land God had promised to them. Consequently, God proclaimed to Moses that He would forgive them, but they would not be allowed to enter the Promised Land.

Today's scripture makes us aware of two important truths: (a) the failure of the Israelites of the Old Testament to believe that what God said did not cancel His promise, and (b) God's Word must be joined with faith *and* action in order to be of value to us.

2. *a.* Copy a dictionary definition of "faith."

b. Add a dictionary definition of "believe."

Here is a great definition of faith: "The gift of God resulting in the capacity to believe that which we cannot see and to act upon that belief."[1] For God's Word to be a vital part of our communion with Him, it must influence our behavior and be combined with faith.

William Barclay's translation of Hebrews 4:2 says, "But the word which they heard was no good to them, because it did not become woven into the very fibre of their being through faith."[2]

3. Read James 2:19-23.

a. What do the demons (agents of the devil) believe?

b. What two aspects of Abraham's life worked together? (See verse 22.)

c. How was Abraham's faith made complete? (See verse 22.)

d. Record verse 24.

MEMORY CHALLENGE

Jeremiah 6:16

This is what the LORD says: Stand at the crossroads and look; ask for the ancient paths, ask where the good way is, and walk in it, and you will find rest for your souls.

4. A promise is only as good as the ability and willingness of the one making it to fulfill it. Read Romans 4:18-21. Record verse 21.

What an assurance that is! Just as we expect God to keep His promises, our word should be regarded by our friends and family as reliable. It is only as our faith and actions together back up our testimony of a relationship with Jesus that the world around us is touched in meaningful ways.

Perfect Rest

Read Hebrews 4:1-11.

1. Record the first portions of Hebrews 4:1 and 11 as one sentence.

The story of the children of Israel in the Old Testament is one of contrasts: sinfulness and righteousness, repentant and "stiff-necked," feast and famine, love and hate. It also is an account of obedience and rebellion. Egypt was a land of hardship and slavery for the Israelites, and we read in Hebrews 3 that the children of Israel grumbled and complained constantly. The land of Canaan was promised to be just the opposite. Canaan was designated to replace the wanderings and unrest of Egypt, but the people had no faith that God would lead them there safely.

God had chosen Canaan to be their "land of rest." Chapters 13 and 14 of Numbers record the sending of 12 spies (one from each tribe) to Canaan to determine the best way to claim the territory. Ten of the men came back with negative reports and tales of giants too big to conquer. God was angered by their lack of faith and determined that none of them except Joshua and Caleb, who believed the obstacles were not insurmountable, would enter the Promised Land.

The Bible makes it clear that for the children of God there *is* a literal experience of rest. God has promised a rest to those who believe and obey.

2. The promise still stands. Record Matthew 11:28-29.

3. Read Isaiah 30:15. This verse says our salvation is in
   _____ and _____ and our strength in
   _____ and _____.

   Contrast this with eternal life in hell, from Revelation 14:11.

4. Some Bible scholars believe a great part of the "rest" God has for us is rest from guilt. From your own life experiences or those you have observed, list some results of guilt:

God is love. Therefore, His Word says, His promise of soul-rest still exists. He will give rest to the guilt-ridden and to those who repent of sin. Though the children of Israel missed Canaan, the promise God made to them is still good, but it is our responsibility to hear His voice.

5. How can we make sure we hear God?

Many times children develop a deaf ear to things said by parents—threats of punishment for bad behavior, for instance. Children have a marvelous capacity for tuning us out. In a sense, this is a spiritual danger also.

6. How can we make sure we do not allow Satan to deafen our ears? Read James 4:7.

It is a wonderful thing to have a vital, abiding relationship with our God. But we must remember that one necessity for victory in spiritual welfare is to listen intently to His voice, carefully obeying His instructions. It is in this daily practice that we truly have "rest in the rest"!

Because rejecting God costs such a price, God wants everyone to repent, believe, and enter into His rest.

7. Read Isaiah 57:20-21.

   a. What are the wicked like?

   b. What does God say of them?

   c. Record Hebrews 4:9.

Jeremiah 6:16 is a wonderful instruction: "This is what the LORD says: 'Stand at the crossroads and look; ask for the ancient paths, ask where the good way is, and walk in it, and you will find rest for your souls.'"

MEMORY CHALLENGE

Memory verse: Copy the verse on a large piece of paper. Cut it into several pieces, making a variety of shapes. Put it back together as a puzzle.

The Word, Alive and Well!

Read Hebrews 4:12.

1. Record the first sentence of Hebrews 4:12.

Underline two important words.

Verse 12 is a little lengthy, but it may be said that the first sentence makes possible the remaining parts of the verse. The description of just what the Word of God does in our lives is very important, but its effect is possible only if the Word remains "living and active."

"Two sources of strength are available to you to assure your success in reaching your full potential in Christ. They are the Word of God and the Holy Spirit."[1]

The ministry of the Holy Spirit is vital to us!

2. *a.* Read 1 Corinthians 2:10. Record the last sentence.

In the Gospel of John, the writer stresses the importance of the Holy Spirit in learning of God and growing in Him.

   b. Read John 6:63. Who gives life to us?

   c. What two things are God's words to us?

3. Second Timothy 3:16 says all Scripture is God-breathed and is useful for at least four things. What are they?

_____ _____

_____ _____

God's Word is not intended just to lie somewhere on a shelf or on a coffee table. That's where many may place it, but God said we should keep it "active." That means we should make it the core of our relationship with Him. From there it will overflow to our whole being.

4. Read 1 Peter 1:23-25.
   a. How are we born again? (See verse 23.)

   b. What great stability is ours? (See verse 25.)

   c. Record Matthew 24:35.

When God's Word is heard, it becomes very personal. It is living, active, sharp, and penetrating, judging the thoughts and attitudes of the heart. What a wonderful formula for molding ourselves into the exact individual child of God that He wants us to be! We need only to be available. The simplest way to hear God's Word is to be prepared to listen.

"Dialogue requires two basic participants: a speaker and a listener. For effective dialogue, the roles of speaker and listener must be passed back and forth between the participants. Effective dialogue occurs when you allow God to talk to you through Bible reading, and you then respond back to Him through prayer."[2]

It is in this practice that the Word of God "judges the thoughts and attitudes of the heart" (verse 12).

Nothing produces Christian maturity and confidence more than this formula, because as today's scripture says, the two-edged sword that cuts through both soft and hard material is *never* inadequate.

When we allow God to use His "sword" on us, "we get inside knowledge about ourselves. It belongs to the most painful experiences of men that they do not know themselves. . . . God alone knows us in such a way as we really are. And when He gives us clarity about ourselves (and He does that through His Word) only then do we know who we are and what we are."[3]

Today's scripture says God's Word "judges the thoughts and attitudes of the heart." The following are the words to a very special hymn. With your Bible in your hands, pray these words:

> *Search me, O God, and know my heart today.*
> *Try me, O Savior; know my thoughts, I pray;*
> *See if there be some wicked way in me;*
> *Cleanse me from every sin, and set me free.*
>
> . . . .
>
> *Lord, take my life and make it wholly Thine;*
> *Fill my poor heart with Thy great love divine.*
> *Take all my will, my passion, self, and pride.*
> *I now surrender; Lord, in me abide.*
> —J. Edwin Orr

MEMORY CHALLENGE

Write the memory verse on a Post-it note and attach it on your refrigerator door.

DAY FOUR

God Sees

Read Hebrews 4:13.

1. From Hebrews 4:13, complete these sentences:

   Nothing in all creation is _____

   _____ _____ _____.

   Everything is _____ _____

   _____ _____.

   He is the One to whom we must _____

   _____.

2. Record Psalm 34:15.

3. Record Proverbs 5:21.

God is an all-seeing God. It is hard for us to fully understand how that can be. Oh, we of the 21st century know how to view scenes from all over the world, but we cannot do so without the electronics of our day. Humanity's natural vision can take in only the immediate surroundings of people, places, and things.

4. In contrast, the Bible tells us two important facts about God.

   I. Nothing is hidden from God's sight.
   a. Record Proverbs 15:3.

   b. Read Isaiah 29:15.

   Who does the Lord speak "woe" to?

   c. What two questions do these people ask foolishly?

d. God is speaking in Jeremiah 16:17. Record His words.

II. God sees things as they really are.

Today's verse says everything is "uncovered" and "laid bare." The Greek phrase for these words means to be stripped of all outward coverings so that God sees us "naked." No disguise!

a. Read Psalm 11:4. Where is God observing from?

b. How does He examine what He sees?

Last, Hebrews 4:13 ends by saying we must give account to God. This is one of the most sobering phrases in all the Bible. We are going to be held accountable. Everything will be laid bare before Him, even the thoughts and attitudes of our heart.

5. Read Romans 2:5-11.

a. What two specific sins are listed here by Paul? (See verse 5.)

_____ and an _____
_____

b. How will God judge? (See verse 6.)

I inherited from my father a love for professional baseball. We didn't have the opportunity to actually go to the games, but we always listened to them on radio and then watched them on the "tube." That's how I first heard the expression "the eye in the sky." I learned that all professional teams have an employee whose job is to sit at the highest point in the stadium to watch the game. From there he communicates strategy to the coach in the dugout. Because of his position, the "eye in the sky" has a much broader perspective of what's going on. Remember that God indeed sees the big picture. He sees the heart. He sees the problem. He sees when we are in trouble. Best of all, He *knows* what to do. Let Him do it!

MEMORY CHALLENGE

Quote the memory verse to someone on the telephone, and make a comment about it.

DAY FIVE

Jesus: The High Priest

Read Hebrews 4:14-15.

1. Record Hebrews 4:14.

Hebrews 4:13 ends with a very sobering fact: *everything* is laid uncovered before Him. The King James Version of the Bible says we stand before the eyes of *him with whom we have to do.* In other words, we will have some explaining to do! We will deal with God himself. And so the writer says in verse 14 that it is important to know that we do not stand before God alone. As the legal profession would say, "You have some counsel." And a mighty one He is. Jesus himself is our Advocate. Obviously, He has some great credentials!

He is our great High Priest. The creation of the office of high priest and the listing of his duties come from the Old Testament.

2. *a.* Record Leviticus 16:32-33.

b. Read verse 34. How often was the atonement to be made?

c. What was the atonement to be made for?

d. How long was this ordinance supposed to be observed?

Jesus is the *great* High Priest. This description does not mean "great" in terms of majesty and power, although He is both. It means His particular qualifications to be the

High Priest far surpass any of an earthly high priest. He has experienced all that we humans have. He was the victim of an unjust death. He has been tempted in every way imaginable, and yet without sin. And one of the ways Jesus so effectively silenced and defeated Satan was by quoting the holy Scriptures to him.

3. Read Matthew 4:1-11. Record the three scriptures that Jesus referred to:

Verse 4:

Verse 7:

Verse 10:

Jesus knew how to deal with temptation. He was "tempted in every way." The devil pulled out all the stops with Jesus, and Jesus withstood him. The obvious lesson for us is that it is to our great advantage to know the Word of God in order to resist Satan and his approaches to us.

It isn't just the believer who wrestles with temptation. Everyone confronts moral decisions on a daily basis—in the workplace, at home, at school—almost any time and place. Certainly God blesses us with many pleasant experiences. He provides many reasons for us to give thanks. But we also confront, day after day, situations that present challenges and difficult choices.

4. *a.* From a dictionary, write a definition of "conflict."

b. Write a definition of "choice."

Whatever the conflict, Jesus has set the example of facing temptation and being more than a conqueror. And because He made the right choices, we have a High Priest who is more than able to sustain us, lead us, and bring us through life with victory.

1 John 5:5 clarifies the power needed to deal with conflict: *Who is it that overcomes the world? Only he who believes that Jesus is the Son of God.*

5. Record Revelation 21:7.

And all God's people said "Amen!"—and a hearty "Praise the Lord!"

MEMORY CHALLENGE

Write your own definition of "the good way."

At the Throne

Read Hebrews 4:16.

The verses we have studied the first five days of Lesson 6 can be called "theological," which is basically the study of God and His words. Today's study can be called "practical" because it is the application of what we have learned. Today's scripture is only one sentence (in the NIV), but what a sentence!

1. Record the first phrase of Hebrews 4:16.

The beginning of this text says "let us *then* approach" (emphasis added), which means that because of what has just been said, we may go to the throne of God "with confidence." So we do well to remind ourselves of all that has been said. Let's review:

　a. We do not have an inferior priest.

　b. We have a High Priest who is able to sympathize with our _____ (verse 15).

　c. Our High Priest has been _____ in _____ _____, just as we are (verse 15).

　d. He is one without _____ (verse 15).

The writer says we may approach Him with confidence because He has "been there, done that." He knows and understands our condition. We should not be afraid.

A throne can be intimidating. But this one is unique in many ways.

2. Read Proverbs 20:28.

　a. What two qualities secure a king's throne?

　b. What does Psalm 62:12 say our King is?

　c. How does Hebrews 3:2 describe Jesus?

The throne of our Savior is not intimidating because of who He is.

　d. Record Ephesians 3:12.

3. This throne is a throne of grace! It is occupied by Jesus, our great High Priest. Record John 5:22.

We should and can come with confidence. I love this dictionary illustration of the use of the word "confidence" —"with full *confidence* of victory."[1]

If we have asked Jesus to forgive our sins, we must not fear the throne of God. It welcomes us with the open arms of the Savior. We find forgiveness at the foot of the Cross," and we find grace and mercy at the throne to help us with our needs.

4. Record the second phrase of Hebrews 4:16.

"The term 'mercy' refers more especially to the pardon of sins, while 'grace' is that which we seek to purify the heart and uphold us in all the trials and disappointments of life. . . . How good to know that, when in trouble and sorrow we cry for help, our great High Priest, full of sympathy and compassion, hastens to our side and never fails to give grace in time of need."[2]

"Because of our High Priest's sympathy, we can come with confidence to His throne. It is a throne of grace. There we obtain mercy . . . a reference to forgiveness for the past . . . and grace to help in time of need . . . a reference to the future."[3]

5. *a.* Record the words of praise in Revelation 7:10.

　b. Complete these phrases from Revelation 7:17:

For the _____ at the _____ of the _____ will be their _____; he will _____ them to _____ of _____ _____. And _____ will _____ _____ every _____ from their _____.

There is forgiveness, comfort, understanding, peace, and fellowship at the throne. Whatever you need today, the Lamb of God (Jesus, our Savior) will provide.

Recite the memory verse to the Lord, and thank Him for soul rest.

Hebrews

LESSON 7

■ A Study of Hebrews 5:1-14

Jesus, the Great High Priest

Read Hebrews 5:1-14, concentrating on verses 1-6.

1. Record Hebrews 5:1.

In this verse the Hebrews writer is describing the Jewish high priest. Today, the word "priest" does not specify any particular sect, religion, or gender. *The World Book Dictionary* defines a priest as "a clergyman or minister of a Christian church; a clergyman authorized to administer the sacraments and pronounce absolution." This title is also synonymous with "pastor," "rabbi," "bishop," or "prelate," to name a few. The important factor is that this is someone who connects humanity to God. The writer to the Hebrews used this term in referring to Jesus because he wanted to tie the prophecies of the Old Testament to the New Testament setting.[1]

2. Verse 1 says a priest is to be selected from among the people. Fill in the additional descriptions of his duties:

   a. Verse 1—He is _____ to _____ them [the people] in _____ related to _____;

   b. Verse 2—He is to deal _____ with those who are _____ and are _____ _____.

   c. Verse 4—He must be _____ by _____.

Ephesians 2:17-18 describes part of the mission of Jesus' earthly life. Verse 17 says, *He came and preached peace to you who were far away and peace to those who were near.* This distinction had nothing to do with their actual place of residence but rather to where they were spiritually. Some were "closer" to accepting the truth than others. In verse 18 Paul makes the point that regardless of our spiritual position, near or far, we have the privilege of knowing the priesthood of Jesus.

3. Record Ephesians 2:18.

The 17th chapter of John's Gospel is regarded as one of the "classic" passages of the New Testament. It is called the "High Priestly prayer" because Jesus, who would soon be facing His accusers and captors, was praying to God the Father.

4. Read John 17:1-18.

   a. What does Jesus ask of the Father? (See verse 1.)

James 4:7-8

Submit yourselves, then, to God. Resist the devil, and he will flee from you. Come near to God and he will come near to you.

b. To whom did Jesus reveal the Father? (See verse 6.)

c. What do they know? (See verse 7.)

d. What did Jesus give the disciples? (See verse 8.)

e. What does Jesus ask God to do for them through the power of His name? (See verse 11.)

f. What does Jesus want His believers to have? (See verse 13.)

g. Jesus prays for a better alternative than for His followers to be taken out of the world. What is it? (See verse 15.)

h. Record verse 17.

By His own prayer Jesus defined the true responsibilities of the priest. He reminds the Father that (1) He brought them gently to a knowledge of the Father, (2) He has represented His earthly believers in godly matters, and (3) His work has been ordained by the Father.

We may claim Christ as our High Priest. He leads us. He teaches us. He intercedes for us because He has access to the Father. How meaningful to know we can trust Him as our High Priest!

The Submissive Son

Read Hebrews 5:7.

1. Read Hebrews 5:7. This verse tells us about Jesus as He prayed: *He offered up _____ and _____ with loud _____ and _____.*

One of the startling realizations in the New Testament concerning the life of Jesus is that He, too, had to have an active prayer life. We know He was always part of the Godhead. But He came in human form not only to set an example for us of how to live but also to teach the necessity of openness and communication with the Father. Jesus knew that only as He submitted to the Father would His followers, by His example, be able to sustain their salvation after He was gone.

Jesus prayed. And as He did, He set the example and pattern for us. His prayers were of the usual kind: thanksgiving, praise, concerns, seeking guidance, including "petitions," or requests for specific things.

2. Luke records several of the times when Jesus prayed. They were important occasions.

a. Read Luke 3:21-22. What was the event?

b. Read Luke 6:12-16. What important step did Jesus take after praying?

c. Read Luke 9:28-29. These verses record what is called the "Transfiguration." Record verse 29.

d. Read Luke 11:1-2. What request did the disciples make of Jesus?

e. What well-known and meaningful pattern for prayer did Jesus give?

3. Jesus knew the ideal situation for praying. Record Matthew 14:23.

Mark 1:35 says, *Very early in the morning, while it was still dark, Jesus got up, left the house and went off to a solitary place, where he prayed.* This is such an example for us! We often find it difficult to get alone to pray. Our lives seem to be so full of responsibilities and "busyness." Of course, God hears us anytime. But nothing compares with the "on purpose" prayer times when we kneel before Him alone. This takes planning.

4. In the space provided here, list some obstacles we face in developing this vital prayer time.

If you struggle with any of these, prayerfully ask God to help you be an "overcomer of the obstacles"!

Jesus was always mindful (as we should be) to thank the Father for answered prayer.

5. Record the words of Jesus to the Father in John 11:41.

Read again Hebrews 5:7. It closes with one of the most significant phrases in the whole Bible. The first part of the verse tells us how Jesus prayed. A study of the prayers of Jesus assures us that His prayers were heard and answered.

6. According to the last phrase of this verse, why was Jesus heard?

All of us have a desire to know the Savior better. Our prayer life is the surest and most productive way by which to do that. Jesus set the example. His prayers were bathed in His great desire to do the Father's will. But that will was not always the easy way. If we truly want God to hear us, we must follow the Master's example and be "reverently submissive."

MEMORY CHALLENGE

Copy the memory verse on a blank piece of paper. Underline what you feel are key words.

DAY THREE

The Suffering Savior

Read Hebrews 5:8.

1. Record Hebrews 5:8.

What a privilege to be a child of God! Jesus was a child of God. In Hebrews 5:5 God verified His relationship with Jesus: *You are my Son; today I have become your Father.* Ideally, a father bestows upon the child all the goodness and privileges that are within his power to give. A wise earthly father, out of his love for his child, must be willing that his offspring also learn the difficult lessons of life. God the Father allowed Jesus to suffer humiliation, unjust treatment, alienation, and cruelty from His enemies, including a whole realm of indignations that would do most of us in. William Neil wrote, "What Jesus learned by bitter experience was that true obedience entails suffering."[1]

A child usually enjoys protection from harm by his or her parents. In the case of Jesus, we might suppose that His relationship to the omnipotent Father would dictate a life of ease, success, and shelter from persecution and suffering. Not so. There was no exception from suffering because He was a Son.

Jesus suffered. That truth is a mystery to some who question why the Son of God would have to suffer. In speaking of Jesus in his second letter, Peter refers to the "divine power" of Jesus. The temptation to discount Jesus' suffering often comes from the question "If He was divine, why did He have to suffer?" In fact, the Gospels record that He was taunted with just such an implication by some who wished to discount His divinity because of His suffering.

2. Read Luke 23:35. The people watched the Crucifixion and sneered at Jesus. Record their statement in verse 35

Jesus constantly taught the great principles of moral and ethical behavior. He taught by both word and action. He spoke about "turning the other cheek."

3. *a.* Record the first sentence of 1 Peter 2:23.

b. He taught by instruction. Fill in the following spaces from Luke 6:27-28:

_____ *your enemies* (verse 27).

_____ _____ *to those who hate you* (verse 27).

_____ *those who curse you* (verse 28).

_____*for those who mistreat you* (verse 28).

Besides physical suffering, well documented in the Crucifixion account, Christ suffered excruciating mental agony. He was degraded by rich and poor, the powerful and the peasant, the pious and the infidel.

We as His children are not exempt from similar distress, insult, and even physical harm. However, our comfort is assured in Romans 8:17.

4. Complete this sentence from that verse: *Now if we are children, then we are heirs—heirs of God and co-heirs with Christ,* _____ _____ _____

_____ _____ _____ _____

_____ _____ _____ _____

_____ _____ .

5. Philippians 3:10-11 is a real challenge to those who follow in His footsteps. It states a very fervent desire to be like Jesus. Complete these meaningful verses: *I want to* _____ _____ *and the* _____ *of his* _____ *and the* _____ *of sharing in his* _____ , *becoming* _____ _____ *in* _____ _____ , *and so, somehow, to* _____ *to the* _____ *from the* _____ .

Jesus was subjected to both mental and physical stress. "He acquired the actual experience of what it means to obey in circumstances of overwhelming distress; unspeakable sufferings were accumulated upon His head near the close. His heart was overwhelmed with agony at the prospect, but He never once wavered in His obedience to God."[2]

To follow in the Master's footsteps means a willingness to follow in His suffering. William Barclay wrote, "There is no door through which tears do not pass."[3] The door of obedience will lead us at times to suffering. If we wish to participate in His glory and victory, we must be willing to follow His example of obedience!

MEMORY CHALLENGE	**DAY FOUR**

Write the verse by memory on a sheet of paper.

Growing Up

Read Hebrews 5:11-13.

1. Read Hebrews 5:11-12.

   a. Why does the writer say he hesitates to tell them more? (See verse 11.)

   b. What does this verse say they should already be? (See verse 12.)

   c. Instead, what do they still need? (See verse 12.)

   d. The one who lives on milk stays an _____. (See verse 13.)

   e. What teaching comes when a person advances beyond milk? (See verse 13.)

   The people addressed in these verses were Jews. As such, they had been taught the Old Testament scriptures. Having accepted Christ, they now knew those teachings had been completed by the coming of the Messiah. With that knowledge and experience, the writer of Hebrews scolded them mildly, because they had not embraced the great opportunity to mature in their spirituality.

   The Hebrews writer knew that for these new Christians, understanding the new faith did not always come easily. "The full orb of the Christian faith is by no means an easy thing to grasp, nor can it be learned in a day. It takes time to teach, and it takes effort to learn. Second, the hearing of his hearers is dull. The writer to the Hebrews did not shirk to bring to men his message, even if his message was difficult. He regarded it as his supreme responsibility to pass on the truth he knew."[1]

   Remember Peter Pan, the boy who refused to grow up? He was just an imaginary person, so he could refuse to grow up. But in the real world, there are undesirable consequences for those who *can* grow up but *refuse* to do so. The same is true with spiritual maturity.

2. *a.* Record 1 Peter 2:1.

   b. Record 1 Peter 2:2.

   We should see that verse 1 explains the first step in carrying out verse 2. Petty and malicious behavior is childish.

   Paul writes extensively to the Ephesians about growing up and maturing.

3. Read Ephesians 4:11-13. Verses 7 through 10 have explained that it was Christ who gave people different responsibilities in the Kingdom. All these deeds had a purpose. Record them.

   To _____ God's _____ for
   _____ of _____, so that the
   _____ of Christ may be built up (verse
   12).

   We [may] all reach _____ in the _____
   and in the knowledge of the _____ of God
   and become _____, attaining to the
   _____ measure of the _____ of
   Christ (verse 13).

   Verse 14 says, *Then we will no longer be infants, tossed back and forth by the waves, and blown here and there by every wind of teaching by the cunning and craftiness of men in their deceitful scheming.*

4. Record verse 15.

   The writer of Hebrews does not lament that there are "babes" in the Kingdom. As long as God woos and wins new converts unto himself, there will always be those who are "babes." It is the refusal to become mature that the writer decries!

   A distinguished doctor friend assured me that milk is a good and vital nutrient for newborns, but it is not sufficient by itself to properly develop and sustain the adult body. His words were "The essentials for adulthood are not in milk for the long haul."

5. So just how should we grow?

   Record the first sentence of 2 Peter 3:18.

6. See 2 Thessalonians 1:3. What two things associated with growth does Paul thank God for?

   "God's works are perfect in every stage of their growth. Man's works are never perfect until they are in every respect complete."[2]

   Lord, teach me today. Teach me Your ways. Teach me the meaning of Your words that I may grow in understanding. My desire is to add knowledge and meaning to what I already know about You. I long for daily instruction and guidance from You and Your Word. Thank You!

MEMORY CHALLENGE

Say the memory verse to yourself in a mirror.

Spiritual Maturity Part 1

Read Hebrews 5:13.

1. Record Hebrews 5:13.

We have read in verse 12 that infants need milk. In verse 13 the writer begins to teach us the importance of spiritual growth. Ideally, maturity will follow infancy. "Infancy has its charms, but not as a permanent state. Infancy must pass on by orderly development into manhood. Continuous spiritual infancy is unnatural and sinful."[1]

If we love God, our first desire should be to know Him better. This springs from our reverence for God and His will for us. Jesus knew not only the longing of the human heart but also what would satisfy that longing.

2. Record Matthew 5:6.

Today's verse implies that when we "grow up" spiritually we will be acquainted with righteousness. *The World Book Dictionary* defines "righteous" as "doing right, virtuous, behaving justly."[2] When "-ness" is added to a word, it means "in the state of . . ." Example: "kindness" means "the state of being kind." So when we define "righteous" as "the state of doing right," we can say that righteousness reflects one's inner condition. It goes without saying that to live in the state of being righteous, we must be spiritually mature.

3. Complete 1 John 3:10. *This is how we know who the _____ of God are and who the children of the _____ are: Anyone who does not do what is _____ is not a child of _____; nor is anyone who does not _____ his _____.*

4. The Bible has much to say about righteousness. Read Philippians 3:7-9. Complete verse 9: *[I should not have] a _____ of _____ _____ that comes from _____ _____, but that which is through _____ in _____—the _____ that comes from _____ and is by _____.*

5. As we become as "the righteousness of Jesus," we acquire other qualities that are a part of being "grown up" spiritually.

   a. Summarize 1 Timothy 6:9-10.

   b. Verse 11 says to *flee from all this, and pursue* _____, _____, _____, _____, _____ and _____.

Maturity produces a whole new value system in us.

   c. From a dictionary, write a meaning of "pursue."

6. The underlying reason that we should pursue righteousness is given in 1 Peter 2:24.

   a. Record it here:

   b. Physical maturity develops by properly feeding the _____.

   Mental maturity develops by properly feeding the _____.

   Spiritual maturity develops by properly feeding the _____.

What we do with our mind and what we feed it will determine our spiritual health and the degree of importance our pursuit of Jesus Christ and His righteousness is to us.

My grandmother was a saint in an apron. She really knew the Lord! I think of her often at mealtime. When Grandma was with us for a meal, we insisted she pray—because she talked to the Lord in such a personal way. At the end of her prayer she always finished with "Feed our souls with the bread of life." I have come to realize what a meaningful and important expression that is. She knew that the feeding of our spiritual beings was much more important than the feeding of our physical bodies. That's how we ultimately mature. That's how we grow to the full state of righteousness!

7. Where are you in your spiritual journey? Are you maturing? In a quiet time with the Lord, ask Him to help you evaluate your walk with Him.

MEMORY CHALLENGE

Fill in the blanks: _____ yourselves, then, to _____. _____ the _____, and he will _____ from you. Come _____ to God and he will _____ _____ to you.

James 4:7-8

Spiritual Maturity Part 2

Read Hebrews 5:14.

1. Record Hebrews 5:14.

    Solid food is for the mature. 1 Corinthians 13 is called the "love chapter" because it is the scriptural standard for what love is. Verse 11 indicates that this kind of love is mature: beyond childishness.

2. It says,

    When I was a _____, I _____ like a child. I _____ like a child, I _____ like a child. When I became a man [mature], I put childish ways behind me.

    Then my life will reflect the behavior of a mature adult.

3. Read today's verse again. Those who are mature have _____ themselves.

    God's Word gives specific instruction about how to be a victorious Christian. One reason we need to read it is to discover what God expects of us and how we can integrate those things into our daily lives.

    In chapter 13 of John's Gospel we read the account of Jesus and His disciples in the Upper Room just before the Crucifixion. Here Jesus washed the disciples' feet to demonstrate humility and the meaning of servanthood.

4. Read John 13:12-17. Record verses 15 and 17 together.

    Jesus knew the apprehension among His disciples when He spoke of His impending death. To them it seemed their foundation was crumbling. Jesus allayed their fears. He said He would not leave them without help and guidance. In John 14:26 Jesus told the disciples the Father would send them the Holy Spirit.

5. What two things will the Holy Spirit do for the followers of Christ?

    Today the promises of Jesus should be the basis of our maturity. He said in John 15:4, *Remain in me, and I will remain in you,* and in John 15:10, *If you obey my commands, you will remain in my love, just as I have obeyed my Father's commands and remain in his love.* Our assignment as mature children of God is to train ourselves by the constant use of God's Word in our own lives and to present it to others by our words and deeds.

    Our training includes being prepared so we are able to distinguish good from evil. Mature Christians make Bible reading a high priority, because it is in God's Word that we find an understanding of good and evil. God says "Thou shalt not" many times in His Word, but the commands and ways to *do good,* to *live righteously,* and to *be Christlike* far outnumber the "Thou shalt nots."

    Our Scripture verse for today states a very important fact. Those who constantly seek solid food are training themselves to recognize the difference between good and evil.

6. 1 John 4:2-3 is a little lengthy but well worth the time to record it:

    Hebrews 5 is a very meaningful and important segment of Scripture. Through the example set by Jesus, we are led to understand the necessity of developing our Christian experience through submission to every circumstance and the vast opportunity to grow in the Lord. Every experience "grows" us a little bit every step of the way.

MEMORY CHALLENGE

Recite the memory verse today to three people.

Hebrews

■ A Study of Hebrews 6

LESSON
8

The Challenge

Read Hebrews 6, focusing on verses 1-3.

Read Hebrews 6:1. The writer urges the reader to move from the elementary teaching about Christ and go on to maturity. Then he lists six things in particular that they have learned.

1. They are—

   a. *not laying again the foundation of _____ _____ acts that lead to _____;*

   b. _____ *in God;*

   c. *instruction about _____;*

   d. *the _____ on of _____;*

   e. *the _____ of the _____;*

   f. *eternal _____.*

These particular truths may not seem elementary to us, but the writer of Hebrews addressed those who had an extensive background, not only of the Old Testament but also in the new salvation by faith in Jesus Christ. He is saying it is "time to move on" to deeper spiritual understanding.

The word translated here as "maturity" is often translated "perfection." Both words capture the true meaning of the original Hebrew word. But does "perfect" necessarily mean "without flaw or error"? That is not at all what the scripture means. Maturity or perfection, as used here, means to live the Christian life with an undivided heart in motive and intent. And this relationship involves body, soul, and spirit.

The apostle Paul wrote a great deal about this mature Christian life.

2. Read Colossians 3:5.

   a. List the aspects of the earthly nature that Paul mentions in this verse: _____ *immorality,* _____, _____, *evil* _____ *and* _____.

   b. These are all classified as _____.

   c. He says to "put to death" these things. List some words you could substitute for "death."

There are attitudes of the soul that are inward as opposed to outward actions. These must also be dealt with. Maturity brings the ability of self-control.

3. a. Record Ephesians 4:26-27.

   b. Paul adds some other advice concerning the mature experience in verses 29-32. What are they? (verse 29)

Jeremiah 6:16

This is what the LORD says: Stand at the crossroads and look; ask for the ancient paths, ask where the good way is, and walk in it, and you will find rest for your souls.

(verse 30)

(verse 31)

(verse 32, first part)

(verse 32, second part)

4. Our spirit is to be perfected and mature.

   a. Read Colossians 3:9-10. What two reasons does the writer give for us not to lie to each other?

   b. *The new self . . . is being* _____ *in* _____ *in the* _____ *of its* _____.

Today's scripture, Hebrews 6:1, urges the believer to mature, to seek a higher plane and a holier walk to bring him or her to maturity. This needs to be the sincere desire of all Christians.

"Our obedience in faith is not the beginning of some vague progress on a shadowy moral way, but is the acceptance of grace, which is always whole, complete, perfect; and in the strength of this encounter our life is lived. 'Perfection' is something belonging to God and coming to us by our contact with God, not as a possession but as a gift."[1]

A Christian's DNA

Read Hebrews 6:4-6.

1. Record Hebrews 6:4 and 6 as one sentence:

This is a much-studied passage of Scripture. Its meaning is often discussed in theological circles. But our first response to it needs to be one of praise or the reminder of the wonderful and blessed relationship the redeemed have with the Savior. We must not miss the lessons that are obvious. Before we take a closer look at what we have just recorded, let us note the privileges and blessings of the Christian.

"Enlightenment"—this word refers to going from darkness to light. Almost all of the New Testament scripture uses this comparison to describe the difference between the sinner and the redeemed, or saved, person.

2. Ephesians 1:18 refers to this comparison.

   a. Record it:

   b. Read Psalm 18:28. What does God do about the darkness?

   c. Read Psalm 19:8. The second part of the verse says, *The* _____ *of the* _____ *are* _____, *giving* _____ *to the* _____.

This refers to an inner condition enjoyed by God's children.

Tastes the heavenly gift. The phrase from Hebrews 6:4 *who have tasted the heavenly gift* causes us to wonder exactly what this gift is. William Barclay says, "The Christian has tasted the *free gift* that comes from heaven. It is only in Christ that a man can be at peace with God. Forgiveness is not something he can ever deserve or merit or win; it is a free gift."[1]

3. See Ephesians 2:8—*For it is by _____ you have been _____, through _____—and this is not from _____, it is the _____ of _____.*

Shares in the Holy Spirit. The ultimate goal and blessing for the believer is to experience the presence of the Holy Spirit, the third member of the Trinity. This gift is for us all. Recorded in Acts 15 is a disagreement between some believers who held that before the Gentiles could experience the Holy Spirit they had to be circumcised. Peter answered (verses 8-9), *God, who knows the heart, showed that he accepted them by giving the Holy Spirit to them, just as he did to us.* Praise the Lord—it is for all of us!

4. Record Romans 5:5.

Who have shared in the Holy Spirit, who have tasted the goodness of the Word of God. The importance of the Word cannot be overemphasized. Romans 10:17 says, *Faith comes from hearing the message, and the message is heard through the word of Christ.*

James concurs in James 1:18: *He chose to give us birth through the word of truth.*

5. Record 1 Peter 1:23.

After experiencing such a wonderful salvation through the agonizing and brutal crucifixion of Jesus, why would anyone turn his or her back on Him? That is precisely the point: God has provided such a magnificent and blessed way of salvation through His only Son that such an act of rejection by someone who had once known the fullness of forgiveness and redemption is unthinkable! And the age-old discussion concerning the meaning of this passage misses one of the most important truths of the Bible: that to know Christ as Savior and then turn one's back on Him (fall away) is to crucify Him anew!

The Hebrews writer "saw the Cross as an event which opened a window into the heart of God. The Cross showed in one moment of time the suffering love which is forever and forever in the heart of God. The Cross said to men: 'That is how I have always loved you and will always love you. This is what your sin does to me and always has done to me and always will do to me.' . . . In God's heart there is forever and ever this agony of suffering and redeeming love. When we sin we crucify Christ again. Sin does not only break God's law; again and again it breaks God's heart."[2] Oh, I do not want to break God's heart!

After typing the preceeding words I took a little break. Walking away from my computer, I found myself singing a chorus I learned as a young teenager. If you know it, add the melody. If not, read it with your own personal emphasis.

I have decided to follow Jesus;
I have decided to follow Jesus;
I have decided to follow Jesus;
No turning back, no turning back.
—Anonymous

MEMORY CHALLENGE

Copy the verse on a large piece of paper. Cut it into several pieces in lots of shapes. Put it back together as a puzzle.

DAY THREE

The Productive Life

Read Hebrews 6:7-8.

1. Today's verses remind us of the basic kinds of lives: the productive one and the useless one. They are described as follows:

   a. Land that _____ in the _____ often falling on it and that _____ a _____ useful to those for whom it is farmed (verse 7). What does this kind receive?

   b. But land that produces _____ and _____ is _____ and is in danger of being _____ (verse 8). What will happen to this land and its crops in the end?

These two verses (7-8) seem to be misplaced. Following Hebrews 6:6 with verses 9-11 would seem to be a more logical sequence. Verses 4-6 and 9-11 deal with actual human activity. In between those two sections are verses 7-8, which tell a parable. Someone has said that a parable is "truth in pictures." It is actually a way to make a point or teach a truth by using an everyday experience as an example. We may remember that Jesus taught many times in this way.

2. Read Matthew 13:1-2.

   a. Why did Jesus get into a boat?

   b. According to verse 3, how did He teach them?

   c. What question did the disciples ask Him in verse 10?

Read His answer in verse 13. On the surface, Jesus seems to be saying that He does not intend for them to understand. But just the opposite is true. They could not easily understand theology, but they could grasp something taught in a manner we would call today an "object lesson."

3. Reread the provisions for a good crop in Hebrews 6:7.

   a. What kind of Christian would you liken to the land in verse 7?

   b. What would that person's spiritual habits probably be?

   c. What personal attitudes would someone like "thorns and thistles" likely have?

In His teachings Jesus frequently used the example of sowing, tending, and harvesting a crop. The majority of the Middle Eastern lands of those days grew crops. The economy of many of them depended on how well the crops were sown, nurtured, and harvested. The land had to be prepared in very careful ways, dealing with the unique soil of the Middle East. The expression in today's verse 7 "drinking in the rain" is very graphic; the ground could become so dry and parched that it seemed the soil actually "drank" itself to production and prosperity. Producing crops took lots of time, personal attention, and labor.

Read Matthew 9:36-38. Jesus again refers to the harvest; but now He is talking about a spiritual harvest. He says to His disciples, *The harvest is plentiful but the workers are few* (verse 37).

4. Record His instructions in verse 38.

In the parable of the sower recorded in Matthew 13, Jesus refers to the dangers of the thorns. In verse 7 He says, *Other seed fell among thorns, which grew up and choked the plants.* We must take seriously the presence of the thorns and thistles. They grow because no one tends to them. Today's Hebrews passage says they are worthless. In the end such land will be burned (verse 8).

5. Record the words of Paul in 2 Corinthians 9:6.

Oh, that we might thirst for the "rain" from the Savior, that we will sow the seeds of the gospel and the good news of Christ's availability to all! It is His great desire that none should perish. To know Him is to be grateful, and from that gratitude should spring seeds of kindness, godliness, and the love of Christ! If we sow, He will give the increase, and we will rejoice in the harvest!

MEMORY CHALLENGE

Memory verse: Write the verse on a Post-it note, and attach it onto the inside of a refrigerator door.

A Godly Standard

Read Hebrews 6:9-12.

1. Record Hebrews 6:10.

After the example of the parable in verses 7-8, the writer assures his readers that God is a God who cares deeply for His creation and by His very nature will treat them fairly. Verse 10 reminds us of one of the great attributes of God himself—He is *just*. *The World Book Dictionary* uses several synonyms for "just"—"right," "fair," "true," and "correct."[1]

What a true description of the nature of God!

2. Read Deuteronomy 32:4. In speaking of God, Moses says, *He is the _____, his works are _____, and all his ways are _____. A _____ God who does no _____; upright and _____ is he.*

3. Read Psalm 89:14. What two things listed here make up the foundation of God's throne?

4. Record Proverbs 21:3.

One very beautiful passage of Scripture prophesying the coming of the Messiah is recorded in Isaiah 9:1-7. The seventh verse says, *He will reign on David's throne and over his kingdom, establishing and upholding it with justice and righteousness from that time on and forever.* In God's value system, justice holds a very high priority!

Read Hebrews 6:10 again. Theologians sometimes describe the Christian life as simply a matter of "being" and "doing"; and though that description seems so simple, it does coincide with biblical teachings. To love is to be loving; to love is to do good deeds!

"If in the midst of all our duties, cares, trials, joys, sorrows, we are not day by day growing in sweetness, in gentleness, in unselfishness, in thoughtfulness, and in all the branches of love, we are not learning the great lesson set for us by our Master in this school of life."[2]

5. *a.* Record Hebrews 6:11.

The writer commends the group he is addressing for their diligence. His desire is that they will continue with this same energy unto the end.

  b. What does he want them to avoid? (See verse 12.)

6. What kind of people does he want them to imitate?

Today's scripture covers so much of what we should be as Christians. Our love for God and a desire to be mature Christians, together with a genuine love and concern for others, is a formula that requires great diligence on our part. One of the greatest truths from God's Word is that He knows our hearts, our motives, our concerns. He alone knows the truth, and it is important to remember that He is just!

7. Romans 12:9-13 is very important, setting a high mark for our lives. Paul says—

_____ *must be sincere. Hate what is _____; cling to what is _____.*

Be _____ to _____ _____ in brotherly _____. Honor one another above _____.

Never be lacking in _____, but keep your _____ _____, serving the Lord.

Be _____ in _____, patient in _____, _____ in prayer.

_____ _____ _____ _____ who are in _____. Practice hospitality.

I have a dear friend who fits the description of these verses. She possesses very few "earthly goods" but has the disposition of a saint and the smile of a very happy, joyous person. One of her friends visited our church, found a relationship with Jesus, and became an active part of the church. One day I asked June what it was that brought her to our church. I wasn't really surprised when she said, "Donna's smile, and her genuine caring for me."

Quote the verse to someone on the telephone, and make a comment about it.

DAY FIVE

When God Promises

Read Hebrews 6:13-15.

1. Record Hebrews 6:15.

In Old Testament times it was considered disgraceful not to have children. To be childless meant one of two things: (1) the "gods" were angry at you, or (2) the true God was punishing you for your sins or those of your ancestors. Furthermore, not to have a son was doubly painful. It was a burden to Abraham that he did not have a son.

God promised Abraham a son. The story is recorded in Genesis. Let's look at the progression:

The promise: *A son coming from your own body will be your heir* (Genesis 15:4).

The fulfillment: *Now the LORD was gracious to Sarah as he had said, and the LORD did for Sarah what he had promised. Sarah became pregnant and bore a son to Abraham in his old age, at the very time God had promised him* (Genesis 21:1-2).

Twenty-five years after God's promise and after leaving the land of Ur, Abraham welcomed the birth of his son Isaac. He had waited all those years for the fulfillment of the promise. During that time he stood firmly on God's promise of a son.

2. One of the most meaningful verses of the Bible is Genesis 15:6. Record it here:

Abraham patiently endured. Perhaps being patient and persevering are two of the most difficult things we do! But together they produce tremendous spiritual results.

3. Read James 1:3-4.

   a. What develops perseverance?

   b. What three results does perseverance bring?

4. In Colossians 1:1-12 Paul tells his readers that he was asking God to give them great spiritual wisdom and understanding. He prays this so they may live a worthy life before the Lord. He desires that they should be strengthened in power according to God's power, which is mighty!

   a. Verses 11-12 say all this is important so the believers may have great _____ and _____, and _____ give _____ to the Father.

   b. In Colossians 2:6-7 Paul lists other positive consequences that follow diligence and endurance—

   rooted and built up in _____

   strengthened in the _____

   overflowing with _____

5. In Luke 8:4-15 Jesus teaches the parable of the sower. In verse 15 He speaks of spiritual reaping:

   The seed on _____ _____ *stands for those with a* _____ *and good heart, who* _____ _____ _____, _____ _____, _____ _____ _____ _____ _____ _____.

When God promises something, you can "take it to the bank." That's an expression that means it's a sure thing. Patience and perseverance are not entirely synonymous, but they go hand in hand while waiting for the fulfillment of God's promise in response to our prayers.

6. Record 2 Timothy 2:12.

Blessed is the man who perseveres under trial, because when he has stood the test, he will receive the crown of life that God has promised to those who love him (James 1:12).

MEMORY CHALLENGE

Quote the verse to someone on the phone, and make a comment about it.

DAY SIX

Hope!

Read Hebrews 6:16-20.

1. Read Hebrews 6:19. We have a hope that is an
   _____ for the _____ and is described
   as _____ and _____.

   God has given us His Word, the Bible. This hope is God's promise that He will keep His Word. This in turn becomes the soul's anchor. In the ancient world the anchor stood for hope. A strong, reliable anchor was regarded as a sure hope for a successful voyage. Pythagoras, a Greek philosopher and religious teacher, said, "Wealth is a weak anchor; fame is still weaker. What then are the anchors which are strong? Wisdom, great-heartedness, courage . . . these are the anchors which no storm can shake."[1] All these qualities are embodied in the anchor of hope the Christian has through salvation. His Word bears that out.

2. Record Romans 15:4.

   An anchor seems like such a small part of a huge ship. In reality, few things are more important. A ship without an anchor on board is always in great danger. In a storm the anchor prevents drifting from the course. In turmoil, without an anchor a ship may be driven to dangerous areas of rocks and underwater debris. In contrast, a ship and its passengers "at anchor" may enjoy the beautiful, sun-soaked areas of the oceans that tourists love so much.

3. There are many reasons to equate hope as our anchor. Record 1 Peter 1:3.

4. Read Titus 1:2. What do faith and knowledge rest on?

5. Read Titus 2:13.

   a. What is the blessed hope?

Scripturally, the anchor also symbolizes a steadfastness that keeps the child of God "calm, cool, and collected" in the time of stress. The psalmist knew that the anchor of hope is a vital part of our peace in the Lord.

   b. In Psalm 119:43 the writer says to his Lord, *I have put my hope in* _____ _____. In both verses 74 and 81 of this psalm he says it again.

6. Read 2 Thessalonians 2:16-17. It says, *May our Lord Jesus Christ himself and God our Father, who* _____ *us and by his grace gave us* _____ _____ *and good* _____, *encourage your hearts and* _____ *you in every good deed and word.*

One of the great chapters of the Bible is 1 Corinthians 13. It is called "the love" chapter because it defines what genuine love really is. In verse 7 it says love always hopes and perseveres. In verse 13 hope is joined with faith and love as a force that will always remain. The impact of hope on individuals and circumstances is immeasurable. Today's verse says it is an anchor for the soul!

Over the years my minister husband and I had the privilege of witnessing the birth of many into the kingdom of God. We experienced the joy of seeing people from all backgrounds and life experiences come to know Jesus as Savior. One of these was a young man who spent six years as a prisoner of war in Hanoi, North Vietnam (now Ho Chi Minh City, Vietnam). Though we didn't know him when he was imprisoned, we were blessed by the way God healed his emotional scars. To this day I cannot imagine being locked in a small room for long periods by myself, with no communication with anyone. Sam (not his real name) told of the awful isolation and longing to talk to someone—anyone. He was not allowed access to radios, television, or reading material. Meals were passed to the prisoners through a narrow opening at the bottom of the bars that kept them captive. I have never forgotten the first time Sam was willing to share all those experiences with us. Don and I sat spellbound listening to the atrocities. We were both speechless. Finally I asked in amazement, "How in the world did you survive that for so many years?" Sam never blinked an eye or paused a moment. "Hope!" he replied.

Fanny Crosby, a wonderful writer of poems and hymns, though born blind, wrote, "Blindness cannot keep the sunlight of hope from the trusting soul!"[2]

The following are words from a hymn written by Priscilla J. Owens in 1882:

> *Will your anchor hold in the storms of life,*
> *When the clouds unfold their wings of strife?*
> *When the strong tides lift, and the cables strain,*
> *Will your anchor drift or firm remain?*
>
> *We have an anchor that keeps the soul*
> *Steadfast and sure while the billows roll,*
> *Fastened to the Rock which cannot move,*
> *Grounded firm and deep in the Savior's love.*

MEMORY CHALLENGE

Recite the verse to the Lord, and thank Him for soul rest.

Hebrews

■ **A Study of Hebrews 7:1-22**

DAY ONE

A Royal Priesthood

Read Hebrews 7:1-22, focusing on verses 1-2.

1. Record Hebrews 7:1.

2. What does verse 2 say His name means?

Perhaps Hebrews 7 is one of the most difficult passages of the Bible to understand. It is rooted in the historical traditions of the Hebrew people. The Bible refers to Melchizedek only 16 times. Five of these are recorded in Genesis, 1 in Psalms—and 11 in the Book of Hebrews.

Melchizedek's main credentials come from his association with Abraham, recorded in Genesis 14. This is the story of Abraham's rescuing Lot, his family, and all their possessions from the king of Sodom. Genesis 14:18-20 records Melchizedek's main appearance in the Bible.

3. *a.* According to Genesis 14, what did he bring to Abraham for the celebration?

   b. What did he bless God Most High for? (See verse 20.)

The reference to Melchizedek by David is found in Psalm 110:4. In this verse God reminds David that his exalted position and communion with his God will not change but will remain as that of Melchizedek.

4. How long is that to be?

Other than his designation as a priest, very little is known about Melchizedek. Most Bible scholars agree on three things about him: (1) "without father and mother" (Hebrews 7:30) does not mean he was not born of natural, earthly parents but that the identity of his parents was not known; (2) by his deep devotion and relationship with God, he had been able to overcome his background and was elevated by God to the position of priest; (3) he was a godly man. Abraham gave him a tenth of everything, and he never would have given tithes to any but a true servant of the living God.

Chapter 6 of Hebrews ends with these words: *Jesus, who went before us, has entered on our behalf. He has become a high priest forever, in the order of Melchizedek.* This suggests that Melchizedek was significant to the Jews as a historical religious figure. It also shows that the writer of Hebrews was a very studious, devout Jew who had accepted the Christ and was anxious to present to the Jewish readers the historical proof that Christ was the Messiah whose credentials they should be familiar with. Jesus was everything the high priest was, but much more—He was King!

His was a *royal* priesthood. Throughout the Bible one way to distinguish a royal leader was by his or her robes. Acts 12:21-23 records an interesting account of the death of King Herod. Though he was wearing his royal robes, his behavior was deceitful. God struck him down, and he was eaten by worms.

MEMORY CHALLENGE

2 Thessalonians 3:16

Now may the Lord of peace himself give you peace at all times and in every way.

5. Why did God punish him?

In contrast, Queen Esther, who always wore her royal robes to enter the presence of the king, exhibited a godly, royal spirit, for which she was honored (Esther 5:1-2).

The royal kingdom of Jesus Christ is the most magnificent of all kingdoms. Its nature is not an outward nobility. True royalty is not an inherited position of authority. "Royal" is an inward quality—it is the *spirit* within.

6. Read John 18:36-37. What does Jesus say would happen if His kingdom were of the world?

The children of God are expected to behave differently than the world. The Christian's behavior needs to be of the "royal" kind!

The following are words from 1 Peter 2:4-5: *As you come to him . . . you also, like living stones, are being built into a spiritual house to be a holy priesthood.*

7. List the descriptions of God's family as recorded in 1 Peter 2:9.

8. Record James 2:8.

Many people refer to the last book of the Bible as "Revelations." The title is not plural. *Revelation* (singular) is the account of conditions and events that will culminate in the coming of Christ, *the* Revelation, recorded in Revelation 19:11. He comes in glory.

9. Record Revelation 19:16.

If we know Christ as Savior, we are a part of His royal family!

> *I once was an outcast stranger on earth,*
> *A sinner by choice and an alien by birth!*
> *But I've been adopted; my name's written down.*
> *I'm heir to a mansion, a robe, and a crown!*
>
> *I'm a child of the King! A child of the King!*
> *With Jesus, my Savior, I'm a child of the King!*
> —Harriet E. Buell

Sing or say the words to this lovely hymn, substituting your name in the appropriate places.

Being Righteous!

Read Hebrews 7:1-2.

1. *a.* Record Hebrews 7:2.

   b. What is the first meaning of the name "Melchizedek"?

Melchizedek is actually a foreshadowing of the priesthood of Jesus. Verse 3 says, *like the Son of God, he remains a priest forever.* "Melchizedek is viewed as a divine mystery breaking into time. He is thereby typical of Christ."[1]

"Melchizedek stands out as a priest-king, not by inheritance or descent, but in his own right. Furthermore, there being no record of the beginning or ending of his kingdom, it becomes a worthy symbol of the eternal priesthood of Christ."[2]

2. The priesthood of both Jesus and Melchizedek is one of righteousness and peace. These two qualities reflect the nature of God. Read Hebrews 1:8-9.

   a. What is the scepter of the Son's kingdom?

   b. What does the Son love?

   c. What does He hate?

Most of us have some reservation about the word "righteous," probably because it sometimes connotes a "holier-than-thou" attitude. The word "righteousness" means the state or condition of being right. The spiritual application indicates a person who is right spiritually. Melchizedek was a king of righteousness because he was "very right" with God. What all of us object to, and what is unacceptable to God, is "*self*-righteousness." That is a conceited, egotistical manner. Some people who have no relationship with God are self-righteous because they have a greatly exaggerated opinion of their own abilities and opinions. To place our confidence in ourselves is to be conceited, which is not acceptable to God.

3. Record 1 John 3:7-8.

4. When we truly know Jesus as Savior, we know we're saved not because of our own merit. Read Titus 3:4-5. The truth of our salvation is found here: *When the _____ and _____ of God our Savior appeared, he _____ us, not because of _____ things we had done, but because of His _____.*

5. *a.* Record Romans 6:18.

In this same passage Paul writes, *Just as you used to offer parts of your body in slavery to impurity and to ever-increasing wickedness, so now offer them in slavery to righteousness leading to holiness* (verse 19).

The World Book Dictionary lists several definitions of a "slave."[3] One is "A person who submits to or follows another." To forsake impurity and to give myself to God as a devoted follower leads me to holiness. What a beautiful and important formula for spiritual victory! Isaiah 61:10 begins, *I delight greatly in the LORD; my soul rejoices in my God.*

b. What two reasons are given in the next two statements of that verse?

6. Read Proverbs 11:18-21, and complete the following statements:

a. He who sows _____ reaps _____ _____ _____ (verse 18).

b. The _____ _____ man attains _____ (verse 19).

c. The wicked will not go _____, but those who are _____ will go _____ (verse 21).

As I was working on today's lesson, I found myself singing this song:

O to be like Thee!
O to be like Thee,
Blessed Redeemer, pure as Thou art!
Come in Thy sweetness; come in Thy fullness,
Stamp Thine own image deep on my heart.
—Thomas O. Chisholm

I have a dear friend whose hobby is "stamping." She makes the most beautiful greeting cards. Those of you who have done this know you can buy stamps of all shapes and forms with just about any image or figure you want to use, and you press their inked patterns onto paper or stationery. She fills hers in with wonderful colors. Sometimes she adds lace or ribbon or cord around the figures. But she *starts with the stamp,* of course. After the outline is in place, the possibilities of creation and embellishment are limitless. In my mind today I see myself as an outline made by God's "stamp." I am praying earnestly that God will fill in the colors and the variations to make me a true stamp of His image. I'm asking Him to add whatever He deems necessary to make me a testimony of His righteousness. Would you join me?

MEMORY CHALLENGE

Fill in the blanks, and then say the verse from memory:
Now may the _____ of _____ himself give you _____ at all times and in _____ way.

2 Thessalonians 3:16

Peace That Lasts

Read Hebrews 7:1-3.

"Peace is not the absence of problems; peace is the presence of God."[1]

1. Paul knew this truth. Read Romans 5:1. Who brings about our peace with God?

2. According to Paul's words in Romans 14:17, what elements make up the kingdom of God?

3. Record Isaiah 32:17.

Today's verses give us an insight into Melchizedek's personal characteristics. His name means "king of righteousness," and the place of his residence means "king of peace." He was a royal king, and his kingdom was one of peace. His righteousness was of peace, not of ceremonial ritual or justice.

In my study of the scriptures concerning these two titles, I discovered a very important insight. Righteousness and peace are connected many times throughout the Bible. It's as if the two are "soul mates"! Both righteousness and peace are cornerstones of God's administration. *The Pulpit Commentary* says, "Righteousness is firm, inflexible, almost stern; peace is mild, merciful, gentle. In the kingdom of our Lord, 'mercy and truth meet together, righteousness and peace kiss each other' (Psalm 85:10)."[2] In the Old Testament, righteousness and peace are the most frequent descriptions of the reign of the coming Messiah. Also, when the two are listed together, almost always peace follows righteousness. William Barclay wrote, "Righteousness must always come before peace. Without righteousness there can be no such thing as peace."[3]

The conclusion is that not only does peace come from God, but it also comes as a product and result of the "rightness" of the heart!

Peace is one of the most sought-after conditions of time. It is desired by nations and individuals. Several years ago there was a splinter group in our nation nicknamed the "Peaceniks." Their agenda was for all humanity to live in peace. For a while it was popular in our nation to greet others or to say good-bye with "Peace!" But because of sin, nations and individuals will never be at peace without a righteousness that comes from God.

"Righteousness is the firm basis for peace. It is true in government as in other things that 'the wisdom that is from above is first pure, then peaceably gentle.' Stable peace is impossible apart from righteousness. Deep craft, subtle diplomacy, strong naval and military forces are miserable guarantees for a nation's peace. The peace and perpetuity of the reign of Messiah are founded upon its truth and righteousness."[4]

4. Read Colossians 1:19-20. Where and how did Christ make peace possible for us?

5. Record Isaiah 53:5.

One great spiritual contribution we can make to our families and our world is the display of personal peace! Peace in the midst of the storm is a great affirmation of our testimony that we know Christ. The Scriptures give us encouraging promises concerning peace.

6. Read Psalm 29:11.

The LORD gives _____ to his people; the LORD _____ his people with _____.

7. *a.* Record Isaiah 26:3.

b. Record Philippians 4:7.

Righteousness and peace go hand in hand. We might call it a classic "Which came first—the chicken or the egg?" situation. Out of righteousness comes peace, and peace becomes a tool for evangelism, which brings righteousness to the repentant heart.

8. Record James 3:18.

Call a friend, and tell him or her you wish this for him or her—then recite the verse.

DAY FOUR

Giving Back

Read Hebrews 7:4-10.

1. Read Hebrews 7:4. Melchizedek was a great man. What fact does the Hebrews writer give to emphasize that?

Abraham was regarded as the great patriarch of the Hebrews, and tithing was a very important priority in the life of the Hebrews. Their descendants were careful to give the required tenth to God. The Hebrews writer was very knowledgeable concerning the history of tithing as it related to obedience, and sometimes to the *dis*obedience of the Jews. It is natural that he would include the matter of giving tithe to God. In today's Scripture lesson tithing is mentioned six times!

The Bible emphasizes the need and requirement for God's people to give generously to His work. The first offering given to God in the Bible is recorded in Genesis 4:3-4, presented by Cain and Abel. Cain was a farmer and gave of his crops. Abel, being a shepherd, gave from his flock. Hundreds of years later is the first mention of *tithing*, found in Genesis 14:20. It was given by Abraham, a very wealthy man. Genesis 13:2 says, *Abram had become very wealthy in livestock and in silver and gold.* In the years between Cain and Abel and Abraham, one very important distinction had been made concerning giving to God: An offering was any amount given to God, but a tithe was defined as one-tenth of the income or increase. In the early Hebrew world the tithe, or tenth, was given from crops, livestock, or whatever else defined a person's assets.

Jacob, Abraham's grandson, knew the importance of honoring God. Genesis 28:10-22 records Jacob's dream from the Lord. In it God showed him that He was going to give him the land he desired and bless him with many descendants. Jacob made promises to God that included his faithfulness in giving back to God.

2. Record Genesis 28:22.

In the Old Testament God assigned various duties to the 12 tribes of Israel. The Levites were to collect the tithes and disperse them according to the needs of God's kingdom.

3. Read Numbers 18:25-29.

   a. What were they to do first with the tithes?

   b. What was the standard for giving to the Lord? (See verse 29.)

Jesus himself "updated" the matter of giving. He emphasized that giving was not to be the product of a legalistic, duty-bound spirit. Giving must be combined with the fruit of the spirit of righteousness. Jesus was stern with the Pharisees and hypocrites.

4. Read Matthew 23:23-24.

   a. What does He say are the more important matters of the Law?

   b. What does He warn against in verse 24?

5. Read Luke 11:42. Jesus does not suggest that they should not tithe.

   a. What does He say the Pharisees neglect?

   b. Record the last sentence of Luke 11:42.

Malachi is the last book of the Old Testament, and Malachi 3:6-12 is one of the most quoted passages of Scripture about giving. The people of God had gotten very lax and neglectful in their giving, but God yearned for His people to restore their relationship with Him. There are several very important questions and statements made by God.

6. Fill in God's words from Malachi 3:

   a. *I the LORD _____ _____ _____* (verse 6).

   b. *Return to _____, and I will _____ to you* (verse 7).

   c. *Will a man _____ _____? Yet you _____ _____* (verse 8).

   d. *But you ask, "_____ _____ _____ _____ _____?"* (verse 8).

e. In _____ and _____ (verse 8).

f. Bring the whole _____ into the storehouse (verse 10).

Verses 10-12: *Test me in this*, says the LORD Almighty, *and*—

1. *See if I will not throw open the floodgates of heaven and pour out so much blessing that you will not have room enough for it* [spiritual blessing];

2. *I will prevent pests from devouring your crops, and the vines in your fields will not cast their fruit* [material blessing].

3. *Then all the nations will call you blessed, for yours will be a delightful land* [social blessing].

7. Record 1 Chronicles 29:9.

Giving is often a controversial subject. God does not want it to be. He will reveal His will for us in this matter. All we must give Him is a listening ear and an open heart.

"When we truly love the Lord with heart, mind, soul, and strength, we are committing our personhood to God. Also, the believer should commit possessions . . . time, talent, and treasure . . . to God. Properly understood, we are not the *owner* but the *manager* . . . the steward . . . of these possessions. When we respond to God by committing back to Him the gifts with which we have been entrusted, we please Him. Such commitment is in the truest sense worship; we are fulfilling the purpose for which we were created."[1]

MEMORY CHALLENGE

Write a short note of appreciation to a friend, and end it with the verse.

DAY FIVE

For Eternity!

Read Hebrews 7:15-17.

1. What is the basis of Christ's priesthood?

Christ's priesthood is very important to our salvation. It is not based on genealogy, law, or power. It is based on His eternal and unchanging nature. His priesthood "is spiritual rather than legal, eternal rather than temporal, abiding rather than changing."[1]

2. *a.* Why is the eternity of Jesus important to us?

b. Record Hebrews 7:25.

The nature of God, His Son, and His kingdom is eternal. And it is because of His nature that we may have eternal life. Jesus spoke to great crowds, often on the shore of the Sea of Galilee. His declaration of eternal life was one of the intriguing things that brought so many to hear Him.

3. Read John 6:40.

a. What two things qualify someone for eternal life?

b. How do we know eternal life will be the result?

4. Record the words of Jesus in John 6:54.

Of course, here Jesus is not requiring the literal eating of His flesh and the drinking of His blood. These are expressions used in that day to emphasize complete identification with someone. "He is saying: 'You must take my life inside you; you must stop thinking of me as a figure in a book and a subject for theological debate; you must take me into you, and you must come into me; and then you will have life, real life.'"[2]

Paul made several references to the eternity of God and consequently the eternity of those who claim Jesus as Lord.

5. Read Romans 1:20.

   a. What two invisible qualities of God does Paul list?

   b. Since these have been clearly seen, Paul says that *men are* _____ _____.

6. Record Romans 6:23.

All of us know the process of human procreation. But no scientist, scholar, researcher, or philosopher has been able to explain the origin of eternity. The best the experts can do is tell us how procreation is achieved and analyze positive potential and probable handicap. The *life* is still God's to give. Just because it now can be put into a test tube, transferred, or sustained by revolutionary methods does not mean it has ever been created by anyone other than God.

At conception a life is committed to eternity. There's no turning back. Oh, there may be a death, but eternity is not erased. One of my brother's parishioners agonized to him, "I have been brought into existence, and I cannot get out!" This is a sobering thought that most of us have had some time or another.

One day out of the blue, our daughter who was seven at the time asked, "What's a soul?" She and my husband were riding together in the car.

After a minute he said, "Susan, do you love me?"

She made a face. "You *know* I love you!"

"How do you know?" he asked.

"I just *do!*"

"Did your nose tell you that?"

"Daddy!"

"Did your hands tell you?"

"Don't be silly!" She was getting a bit impatient.

"Well," Don said, "there's something in you that's called 'spirit.' It's you! But you can't take it out and look at it or touch it with your hands the way you can your knee or your elbow. God has given us each a soul, a spirit, something that is just you, and in your spirit you will live on and on forever and ever. And that is eternity. God is a Spirit, and it is with that inner something in every one of us that we worship Him."

7. Luke 10:25 says a lawyer asked Jesus one of the most important questions ever asked of anyone. "What must I do to inherit eternal life?" Jesus gave him a two-part answer, posed as two questions (verse 26).

   a. Write the questions here:

     1.

     2.

   b. How did the lawyer reply? (See verse 27.)

   "Love the _____ *your* _____ *with all your* _____ *and with all your* _____ *and with all your* _____ *and with all your* _____*"; and, "Love* _____ _____ *as* _____*."*

   c. What were Jesus' two responses to the lawyer's answer?

     1.

     2.

   Eternally Yours, Jesus!

MEMORY CHALLENGE

Each time this verse comes to your mind today, thank the Lord for peace.

Draw Near

Read Hebrews 7:18-22.

1. Record Hebrews 7:19.

Jesus is the hope spoken of in Hebrews 7:19. It is important to remember that the Hebrews writer is writing to a group of very sophisticated Jews. They were Jews who had received and accepted salvation through the death and resurrection of Jesus. The writer was reminding them of the inefficacy of the law. The old priesthood was based almost entirely on physical, outward, and inherited qualifications.

But the new priesthood is based on a life that is indestructible—on Christ's *character, personality, and His being!* Acceptance is now based on inward worth. Jesus gave us direct access to God.

This new priesthood provides a better hope. Sin has always been the main barrier between God and humanity, but Jesus conquered sin on the Cross.

2. Read Titus 3:4-7.

   a. What two words describe the nature of our Savior? (See verse 4.)

   b. Why did He save us? (See verse 5.)

   c. Through whom did our washing of rebirth and renewal come? (See verse 5.)

   d. Record verse 7.

In today's verses God declares a better covenant. The death and resurrection of Jesus provide a better hope, because it is rooted on a better foundation.

3. Read 1 Peter 1:21.

When we believe in God's plan of salvation, that is, the resurrection and glorification of Jesus, our _____ and _____ are in God.

"The bringing in of the better hope has done what the Law could not do. It has made possible the soundness, the wholeness, the integrity of Christian character. . . . It makes possible the righteousness which was the unreachable goal of the ceremonial law."[1]

Jesus did not die to be a martyr. He died and rose again that we may have a hope that is spiritual, reliable, and reachable amid a world that is sinful, selfish, and saturated with despair. I have recently discovered a wonderful book by Philip Yancey. In it he writes, "Because of Easter, I can hope that the tears we shed, the blows we receive, the emotional pain, the heartache over lost friends and loved ones, all these will become memories, like Jesus' scars. Scars never completely go away, but neither do they hurt any longer. We will have re-created bodies, a re-created heaven and earth. We will have a new start, an Easter start."[2]

Yancey also writes, "Because of the cross, I have hope. . . . If God can wrest triumph out of the jaws of apparent defeat, can draw strength from a moment of ultimate weakness, what might God do with the apparent failures and hardships of my own life? . . . Between the cross and the empty tomb hovers the promise of history: hope for the world, and hope for each one of us who lives in it!"[3]

4. The above words give us inspiration to fulfill the words of admonition in 1 Peter 3:15. Record this verse:

I pray this prayer for you today: *May the God of hope fill you with all joy and peace as you trust in him, so that you may overflow with hope by the power of the Holy Spirit* (Romans 15:13).

MEMORY CHALLENGE

If you have family members at home, be sure to say the memory verse to them as they leave for the day, or as you leave them.

Hebrews

LESSON 10

■ **A Study of Hebrews 7—8**

Our Priest, the Savior

Read Hebrews 7:23—8:13, focusing on 7:23-25.

There has long been a debate about who wrote the Book of Hebrews. We do know that this person was a very intellectual person who had great knowledge of theology and a great understanding of the Hebrew language and Jewish traditions. Those who study the writer's words know that he or she clearly loved Jesus as Savior. There is no question that this person had a glorious understanding of the Godhead: the Father, Son, and Holy Spirit. It is God the Father who gave His only begotten Son, and it is the Son who gave His life that we might be saved. The work of the Holy Spirit is to convict and draw people to salvation through Christ.

Read Hebrews 7:25-26.

1. *a.* What is Jesus able to do?

   b. Why is He able to do this?

2. Record 1 John 4:14.

We are reminded again of the words of Paul in Acts 4:12: *Salvation is found in no one else, for there is no other name under heaven given to men by which we must be saved.*

3. Read John 11:25-26. The words of Jesus in verse 25 are *I am the _____ and the _____.* Summarize verses 25-26.

4. Verse 26 of today's Scripture lesson includes some wonderful descriptions of our High Priest.
   ● He is **holy.**
     a. Read the words of the angel to Mary in Luke 1:35. How did the angel describe the baby to be born?

     b. Even the evil spirits knew who Jesus was. According to Mark 1:21-24, who did the possessed man declare Jesus to be?

     c. Record 1 Peter 1:15-16.

Psalm 26:2

Test me, O LORD, and try me, examine my heart and my mind.

- He is **blameless.**
   d. Matthew 27:1-10 records the betrayal of Jesus by Judas. Judas certainly knew the truth concerning Jesus. Record Judas's confession in verse 4.

   e. How is Jesus described in 1 Peter 2:22? (See Isaiah 53:9.)

- He is **pure.**
   f. Read 1 Peter 1:19. How is Jesus described?

   g. Record 1 John 3:5.

   Malachi, in the last book of the Old Testament, prophesies about the coming of Jesus. He writes in verse 3 that He will sit as a refiner and purifier of silver. This is His nature, and His purity will be a standard for His kingdom.

   For all that He is, He is *exalted above the heavens* (Hebrews 7:26). Psalm 99:3 says, *Let them praise your great and awesome name—he is holy.*

   Praise Him! Praise is one of the greatest ways to give back to the Lord. It says to God that we know the source of our salvation and that we give thanks for the sacrifice of the Son that made our redemption possible!

   Praise is not our duty—it is our response!

Once for All!

Read Hebrews 7:26-27.

1. Read Hebrews 7:26-27. Record the last sentence of these verses.

   As we remember that Hebrews was written to the Jews, it is understandable that the background for this statement concerning the sacrifice Jesus made for our sins is found in the Hebrew system of animal sacrifice prescribed by God in the Old Testament. Before the Savior came, atonement for sin was brought about by the sacrificing of certain animals. The Old Testament records very particular requirements for the animals to be used and extensive instructions on the way to sacrifice them. It was a very detailed, sometimes difficult system of atoning for sin.

   In the 21st century, much of the ceremony of the Old Testament is foreign to our thinking and understanding. But whether we understand all that, the Bible makes it clear that Jesus came, lived among us, and gave His life as the ultimate sacrifice for our sins. He became the sacrificial lamb, supplanting once for all the old system of animal sacrifice.

2. Zechariah, a prophet of the Old Testament, prophesied the coming of a Savior who would make the ritual of animal sacrifices null and void. Record Zechariah 13:1.

3. Jeremiah also understood that One would come who would "change the system." Read Jeremiah 31:33. Where did he say God's law would be found in the future?

   "The High Priest which becomes us, or is suitable to our needs, must have a threefold perfection: (1) the perfection of character, (2) the perfection of His offering, and (3) the perfection of intercession. . . . The blood of animal sacrifices, which could never take away sin, was done away in the sacrifice of the body of Christ once for all."[1]

   And now we may come boldly to the throne of God. Paul knew and preached this new access to God.

4. *a.* Record Romans 12:1:

    b. What does Paul say this offering is?

5. Even though Samuel was of early Old Testament times, he knew in his heart the superiority of the offering of ourselves to God. Summarize his words in 1 Samuel 15:22.

    Jesus offered himself. He was the perfect offering, the sacrifice to end all other sacrifices. "Man seeks the presence of God; man is restless until he rests in God; and Jesus alone is the priest who can bring the only offering that can open the way back to God for men."[2]

6. Record Ephesians 5:1-2.

    It was Christmas, and I was eight years old when I received one of the most meaningful gifts I have ever gotten, one I still have. My parents asked me early in October of that year what I would like for Christmas. Instantly I said, "A watch!" I did not know that such things were out of the question for us. My father had a reliable job, but his income was very meager. And in those days you couldn't buy watches just anywhere, only at a jeweler's store, and they cost real money—*lots* of real money. They explained all that to me. So I forgot about it.

    I've never forgotten that Christmas morning. I opened a beautifully wrapped package and found a lovely watch. Imagine my joy! I have never forgotten the best gift of all, however: the look on their faces when I opened that package. As an adult I came to realize the real gift of that moment was not the watch but the tremendous sacrifice they made to bring joy to an eight-year-old daughter! And the joy of their sacrifice was their own Christmas present. God, the Father, stood by as His Son, Jesus, gave His life

that we may have eternal life. The magnificence and meaning of that sacrifice can never be measured. It is joy unspeakable!

MEMORY CHALLENGE

Cut two pieces of paper, each 1" x 2". On one write "HEART" and on the other "MIND." Attach one on each side of your bathroom mirror. Leave them up for the week.

DAY THREE

At the Throne

Read Hebrews 8:1-2.

1. Read Hebrews 8:1-2.

   a. Where is our high priest?

   b. Who set up the true tabernacle?

A review of our study of Hebrews will show that so far the writer has been declaring to the readers just who Jesus is in relation to other important spiritual leaders in their history. Jesus has been shown to be superior to the angels, greater than Moses or Joshua, and a more effective priest than the Levitical priests. He is God, the true High Priest. Here, then, sitting on the throne in heaven we see His glory!

"There can be no glory greater than the glory of the ascended and exalted Jesus. His glory is nothing less than the glory of the majesty of God."[1] Verse 1 seems to say, "of all the things we have spoken, here is the summation."

We cannot imagine the glory and magnificence of His throne and presence. The Book of Psalms often describes this scene of majesty and glory.

2. Read Psalm 29:4.

   a. How is the voice of the Lord described?

   b. What additional descriptions does the psalmist write in Psalm 93:1?

   c. Record Psalm 96:6.

   d. Psalm 104:1 says that God is very _____; he is clothed with _____ and _____.

The majesty and glory of Jesus, the Son, at the throne is wonderful to think of and picture in our minds. But perhaps the more important and spiritual meaning for us is that He serves us there. In all His majesty, righteousness, and beauty, He serves those who call upon Him. The purpose of His glory, in part, is to enable us to enter into that glory. The trials and burdens of our present lives are the "admission ticket" to this throne.

3. Record Revelation 3:21.

Verse 2 of today's Scripture lesson speaks of the true tabernacle as being a sanctuary. At the beginning of Psalm 15, David wrote of this sacred place.

4. *a.* Record Psalm 15:1-2 together.

   b. Read Psalm 27:5. Where does God hide the psalmist in times of trouble?

To accept Christ as Savior not only is an important and beautiful experience but also makes us eligible for His service to us as our High Priest. He intercedes for us at the throne of grace. He knows us as His children, and His attention and care are ours to rely on and enjoy. J. Sidlow Baxter wrote some beautiful words pertaining to today's scripture. He said, "Our glory-robed, sympathetic High Priest and Advocate and Intercessor ministers representatively for us yonder in the heavenly Holy of Holies, bearing our names like jewels on His mighty shoulders and on His gentle bosom."[2]

MEMORY CHALLENGE

Make a drawing of a heart. Inside draw a happy face, and keep it as a marker in your Bible through Day Six.

DAY FOUR

Redeemer and Mediator

Read Hebrews 8:3-6.

1. *a.* According to verse 3, what is the main duty of a high priest?

   b. What is the reason (verse 4) Jesus would not be a priest on earth?

"Jesus could never have been a priest under the Old Testament law. What Jesus does is infinitely beyond what transpired in the earthly Tabernacle. There, gifts and sacrifices are offered continually. Christ's sacrifice was offered but once."[1]

2. What did Jesus offer? (See Hebrews 7:27.)

Jesus gave His life that we might have eternal life. He also gave His life that He might demonstrate the servanthood of His nature to all His followers.

3. *a.* Philippians 2:5-8 describes the attitude of Jesus. According to verse 7, what role did He assume?

   b. Read Matthew 20:18-19. What two reasons are given for Jesus to come to earth?

The death and resurrection of Jesus added the majesty of His holiness to His life of service and made a way for humanity to come to God. In referring to the writer of Hebrews, William Barclay wrote, "Religion to him was access to God; it was fellowship with God; it was the right to enter into the presence of God. Therefore the supreme function of any priest is to open the way to God for men. The priest removes the barriers between God and man."[2]

By His death Jesus guaranteed to you and me that through Him we would always have a "voice" in the Godhead. How exciting and magnificent that Jesus cared so much for us!

Verse 6 of today's scripture calls Jesus the *mediator*. Centuries before this, Job, in the midst of his terrible tribulation and trial, longed for a mediator. He said, *If only there were someone to arbitrate between us [God and humanity]* (Job 9:33).

4. Read Ephesians 2:17-18. Record verse 18.

Jesus as Mediator is in part the meaning of Christ as Redeemer. Humans may actually be brought into communion with God, the divine Being, by way of Jesus, the Redeemed! It is His role as mediator that allows us, mere mortals, to *approach the throne of grace with confidence, so that we may receive mercy and find grace to help us in our time of need* (Hebrews 4:16).

Today's scripture says the ministry of Jesus is founded in part on "better promises." The promises are better not because they are more meaningful or dependable but because now, by His death and resurrection, He has fulfilled all things necessary to make every promise available to everyone, in every circumstance. The promise has become "better" because it is now guaranteed by Jesus' death, resurrection, and ascension.

"It is a mysterious wonder that God the Son *could* die; still more that he *should* die; still more that he would die; and most of all that he *did* die."[3]

5. Record the samples of God's great and better promises:

   a. Psalm 34:19, substituting your name for "a righteous man"

   b. Psalm 138:8 (first phrase)

Paul referred to Abraham in Romans 4:20-21 when he wrote, *He did not waver through unbelief regarding the promise of God, but was strengthened in his faith and gave glory to God, being fully persuaded that God had power to do what he had promised.*

Believe it—He will do it!

MEMORY CHALLENGE

Say the memory verse as a part of your prayer before meals.

A Promise Is a Promise

Read Hebrews 8:7-10, Part 1.

1. Read Hebrews 8:7-10. What did God say He would make?

2. In verse 9, what reason does God give for a new covenant?

We have come to the point in our study of Hebrews at which we need to look at the Bible as a two-part work and understand God's approach to us in this day and age. Most everyone is familiar with the words "Old Testament" and "New Testament"—these are the two main divisions of the Bible. A "testament" is an agreement of importance between two people or groups. In the religious sense it is regarded as a listing of beliefs and/or principles. When we apply this definition to the Bible, we see exactly that. The two divisions contain God's laws and requirements for a relationship with Him and instructions on how to maintain this bond between God and humanity.

In today's scripture we read the word "covenant." Its meaning is almost identical to that of "testament." A covenant is an agreement entered into by two parties and is mostly a promise or promises.

"'Covenant' now becomes a major term in Hebrews. It has been used only once incidentally up to this point. From here on, it is found no less than 16 times. No term is more important in understanding the message of the Bible than this one. It gives the titles to the two major divisions of the entire Bible. The 'Old Testament' is the old covenant; the 'New Testament' is the new covenant."[1]

Biblically, the Old and New Testaments record for us the two distinct ways God dealt with humanity and how He continues to deal with us today. The "Old" is basically historical: the record of creation, God's law, and the system of animal sacrifice for sin. The Greek word here for "new" means new in *quality*. The "New" is a new quality: a person may know God on a one-to-one basis, and that is very personal. Salvation is transacted between God and the individual!

Because Jesus gave His life and rose from the grave, the new covenant does not require animal sacrifice. Salvation no longer comes from an outward sacrifice or offering but is now an internal relationship with a very personal Savior.

3. Read Hebrews 8:10. God says, *I will put my laws in their* _____ *and* _____ *them on their* _____. *I will be their* _____, *and they will be* _____ _____.

4. Paul describes the new message and ministry in 2 Corinthians 3:2-3. He writes of two distinct differences in the new gospel. He says the result of this ministry is now written _____ _____ _____ (verse 2). It is not on _____ _____ _____ but on tablets of _____ _____ (verse 3).

Now we can enjoy direct communication with God. Furthermore, salvation is not restricted to the wise, the rich, the pious, the talented, or any elite or superior group. Nor can it be earned. It is free! In the church of my childhood they called that "shouting material." Amen and amen!

In Matthew 11:25 Jesus says the way of salvation has been revealed to little children. That takes in all of us, because Matthew 18:3 states we must become as children to enter the kingdom of heaven.

5. Thinking about your own childhood or your experience with children, list some childlike qualities you think help us to humble ourselves before God.

We are now to obey God because we love Him, not because of fear of punishment. Our relationship with Him reaches a new covenant level: from emotional fear and incrimination to adoring love and admiration. We give Him our heart, and the heart where the "law" now abides is free to respond without the ritual of animal sacrifice or outward cleansing. That's how we have *victory* in Jesus.

6. Write Psalm 57:7 in your own words.

Let us thank Christ that His death and resurrection provide a new covenant for us that gives us direct access to God through our minds and hearts. The words of 1 Thessalonians 3:13 are my prayer for you and for me: *May he strengthen your hearts so that you will be blameless and holy in the presence of our God and Father when our Lord Jesus comes with all his holy ones.*

"In the first covenant God said, 'Thou shalt not.' Now He says, 'I will!'" (Anonymous)

MEMORY CHALLENGE

Write the letters M, I, N, and D vertically on a piece of paper. Write a word after each letter describing how you would like God to see your spiritual "mind."

DAY SIX

The Great Mind-set

Read Hebrews 8:10-12.

1. Read Hebrews 8:10. As we noted in Day Five, God said the new covenant He was establishing would be written on the heart. Additionally, He would put His laws

   _____ _____ _____.

   The importance and function of the mind as it relates to our relationship with God cannot be overstated. It is here we decide to serve God. Francois Fenelon, a great theologian and philosopher, wrote, "True religion resides solely in the will!"

   I grew up in a wonderful evangelistic church—yet I remember many spiritual "ups and downs." Those were very emotional times. I thank God that He kept me responsive to the tugging at my heart strings. All of us love and respond to the "feelings" of worship when we know and feel God's presence: the "warm-fuzzies," so to speak. These times are absolutely necessary and are high points of our walk with God.

   But I am also grateful for, and can remember very well, when I made up my mind once and for all that I would serve the Lord no matter what. Period! End of discussion. Doubting was no longer an option. I decided to quit trying to figure it all out. Perhaps that is why John 9:24-25 is one of my favorite Scripture passages.

2. Read John 9:24-25, and record the concluding statement of John 9:25.

3. In Romans 8:5-8 the apostle Paul wrote some very enlightening words about the mind.

   a. From verse 5, what is the mind-set of those who live according to the sinful nature?

   b. What do those who live in accordance with the Spirit have their minds set on?

c. What is the result of the person of a sinful mind? (See verse 6.)

d. What two phrases describe the sinful mind? (See verse 7.)

e. What is the result of one who is controlled by the sinful nature? (See verse 8.)

4. Record the last sentence of Hebrews 8:10.

The crowning glory of the new covenant through the Savior's sacrificial death and resurrection is that now personal fellowship with God is not only possible but necessary. The child of God can enjoy an inward assurance of belonging completely to God.

The promise is very simple: those who make up their minds to believe God and live by His precepts will be claimed by Him as His family. He will be God to those who love Him with all their hearts and minds and who keep His commandments. He will be to you and me everything we need!

5. There is another "bottom line" to this relationship. Record Hebrews 8:12.

My family has long teased me about my stubbornness. Well, I *think* they are teasing. I definitely am *not* stubborn! I did think about it one evening when I was preparing dinner for company. I had in my hand a very stubborn package of frozen vegetables. I tugged and tugged and could not get the package opened. My eyes suddenly saw the words on the end I was tugging. They said, "Open other end." No way—I walked across the kitchen, opened a drawer, and took out my scissors. As I cut the plastic bag, I said out loud, "I'll open the end I *want* to open!" I think it was at that moment that I realized why I had such a hard

time letting God put His words in my mind and write them on my heart!

Perhaps the greatest gift I can present to Jesus is an open heart and a determined mind.

MEMORY CHALLENGE

Thank the Lord several times today for His work in your heart and mind.

Notes

Introduction to Hebrews

    1. Quoted in William Barclay, *The Letter to the Hebrews* (Philadelphia: Westminster Press, 1955), 17.

    2. William Barclay, *The Letter to the Hebrews* (Edinburgh, Scotland: St. Andrew Press, 1955), xvii.

    3. H. Orton Wiley, *Epistle to the Hebrews* (Kansas City: Beacon Hill Press, 1959), 13.

    4. Ibid.

Lesson 1, Day 5

    1. William Barclay, *The Letter to the Hebrews* (Philadelphia: Westminster Press, 1976), xv.

Lesson 2, Day 3

    1. Barclay, *The Letter to the Hebrews*, 7.

    2. Adam Clarke, *Clarke's Commentary*, (Nashville: Abingdon-Cokesbury Press, 1977), 6:688.

Lesson 2, Day 5

    1. E. Stanley Jones, *The Unshakeable Kingdom and the Unchanging Person* (Nashville: Abingdon Press, 1970), 31.

Lesson 3, Day 1

    1. *The World Book Dictionary* (Chicago: Doubleday and Co., 1970), s.v. "eternal."

Lesson 3, Day 2

    1. H. Orton Wiley, *Epistle to the Hebrews* (Kansas City: Beacon Hill Press, 1959), 31.

Lesson 3, Day 4

    1. *The World Book Dictionary*, s.v. "salvation," "savior."

    2. Wiley, *Epistle to the Hebrews*, 70.

Lesson 3, Day 6

    1. Johannes Schneider, in *Beacon Bible Expositions* (Kansas City: Beacon Hill Press of Kansas City, 1974), 11:29.

    2. Devotional by Theodore Monod in *Streams in the Desert*, vol. 2 (Grand Rapids: Zondervan Publishing House, 1966), October 1 devotional.

Lesson 4, Day 1

    1. Richard Taylor, in *Beacon Bible Commentary* (Kansas City: Beacon Hill Press of Kansas City, 1967), 10:30.

Lesson 4, Day 2

    1. H. C. G. Moule, *Ephesian Studies* (London: Picker and Inglis, n.d.).

    2. T. W. Willingham, *Spiritual Insights*, Book 7 (Kansas City: Beacon Hill Press of Kansas City, 1987), 11.

Lesson 4, Day 3

    1. Wiley, *Epistle to the Hebrews*, 91.

Lesson 4, Day 5

    1. Wiley, *Epistle to the Hebrews*, 130.

    2. *The World Book Dictionary*, s.v. "slave."

Lesson 4, Day 6

    1. Devotional by Mrs. Charles Cowman in *Streams in the Desert*, Jan. 19 devotional.

Lesson 5, Day 1

    1. Barclay, *The Letter to the Hebrews*, 23.

Lesson 5, Day 2

    1. *The World Book Dictionary*, s.v. "courage."

    2. Wiley, *Epistle to the Hebrews*, 115-16.

Lesson 5, Day 3

    1. *The World Book Dictionary*, s.v. "lawless."

Lesson 5, Day 4

    1. Barclay, *The Letter to the Hebrews*, 26.

Lesson 5, Day 5

    1. Wiley, *Epistle to the Hebrews*, 130.

    2. Lawrence O. Richards, *Expository Dictionary of Bible Words* (Grand Rapids: Zondervan Publishing House, 1985), 184.

    3. Devotional by James McConkey in *Streams in the Desert*, Nov. 4 devotional.

Lesson 6, Day 1

    1. *Today's Disciple* (Kansas City: Beacon Hill Press of Kansas City, 1996), 115.

    2. Barclay, *The Letter to the Hebrews*, 29.

Lesson 6, Day 3

    1. *Today's Disciple*, 23.

    2. Ibid., 29.

    3. W. T. Purkiser, in *Beacon Hill Expositions*, 11:44.

Lesson 6, Day 6

    1. *The World Book Dictionary*, s.v. "confidence."

    2. Wiley, *Epistle to the Hebrews*, 168.

    3. Purkiser, *Beacon Bible Expositions*, 11:47.

Lesson 7, Day 1

    1. *The World Book Dictionary*, s.v. "priest."

Lesson 7, Day 3

    1. William Neil, "Torch Bible Commentaries," in *The Epistle to the Hebrews* (London: SCM Press, 1950), 42.

    2. Lindsay, *Lectures on Holiness*, Quoted in Wiley, *Epistle to the Hebrews*, 187.

    3. Barclay, *The Letter to the Hebrews*, 46.

Lesson 7, Day 4

    1. Barclay, *The Letter to the Hebrews*, 47.

    2. Hannah Whitall Smith, *God Is Enough* (Grand Rapids: Francis Asbury Press of Zondervan Publishing House, 1986), 67.

Lesson 7, Day 5

    1. *Letters to the Hebrews*, vol. 21 of The Pulpit Commentary (Grand Rapids: William B. Eerdmans Publishing Co., 1950), 149.

    2. *World Book Dictionary*, 1970 ed., s.v. "righteous."

Lesson 8, Day 1

1. R. Gregor Smith, "Perfect," *A Theological Word Book of the Bible*, ed. Alan Richardson (London: SCM Press, 1957), 167.

Lesson 8, Day 2

1. Barclay, *The Letter to the Hebrews*, 56.
2. Ibid., 59.

Lesson 8, Day 4

1. *The World Book Dictionary*, s.v. "just."
2. Devotional by J. R. Miller in *Streams in the Desert*, September 2 devotional.

Lesson 8, Day 6

1. Barclay, *The Letter to the Hebrews*, 63.
2. *A Treasury of Wisdom*, comp. Ken and Angela Abraham (Uhrichsville, Oh.: Barbour and Co., 1996), May 9 devotional.

Lesson 9, Day 2

1. Purkiser, *Beacon Bible Expositions*, 11:58.
2. Wiley, *Epistle to the Hebrews*, 232.
3. *The World Book Dictionary*, s.v. "slave."

Lesson 9, Day 3

1. H. B. London Jr. and Stan Toler, *The Minister's Little Devotional Book* (Tulsa, Okla.: Honor Books, 1997), 142.
2. *Letters to the Hebrews*, 192.
3. Barclay, *The Letter to the Hebrews*, 75.
4. *Letters to the Hebrews*, 192.

Lesson 9, Day 4

1. W. Donald Wellman, *Today's Disciple*, Discipleship Series, 4th ed. (Kansas City: Beacon Hill Press of Kansas City, 1996), 160.

Lesson 9, Day 5

1. Purkiser, *Beacon Bible Expositions*, 11:60.
2. William Barclay, *The Gospel of John* (Philadelphia: Westminster Press, 1975), 1:231.

Lesson 9, Day 6

1. Purkiser, in *Beacon Bible Expositions*, 11:62.
2. Philip Yancey, *The Jesus I Never Knew* (Grand Rapids: Zondervan Publishing Company, 1995), 219.
3. Ibid., 274.

Lesson 10, Day 2

1. Wiley, *Epistle to the Hebrews*, 256.
2. Barclay, *The Letter to the Hebrews*, 92.

Lesson 10, Day 3

1. Barclay, *The Letter to the Hebrews*, 93.
2. Baxter, *Awake, My Heart*, 128.

Lesson 10, Day 4

1. Purkiser, *Beacon Bible Expositions*, 11:65.
2. Barclay, *The Letter to the Hebrews*, 94.
3. Baxter, *Awake, My Heart*, 103.

Lesson 10, Day 5

1. Purkiser, *Beacon Bible Expositions*, 11:65.

Wisdom Notes*

_____
_____
_____
_____
_____
_____
_____
_____
_____
_____
_____
_____
_____
_____
_____
_____
_____
_____
_____
_____
_____
_____
_____
_____
_____
_____
_____

Wisdom Notes*

Date _____

Book _____

Lesson No. _____

Scripture Ref. _____

_____

_____

_____

_____

_____

_____

_____

_____

_____

_____

_____

_____

_____

_____

_____

_____

_____

_____

_____

_____

_____

_____

_____

_____

_____

_____

_____

_____

_____

_____

*You may make copies of this sheet to use for note taking as you work through the lessons of this Bible study.

Prayer Requests for Small Groups

Date _____

Name: _____

    Request: _____

Name: _____

    Request: _____

Name: _____

    Request: _____

Name: _____

    Request: _____

Name: _____

    Request: _____

Name: _____

    Request: _____

Name: _____

    Request: _____

Name: _____

    Request: _____

Prayer Requests for Small Groups

Date _____

Name: _____

    Request: _____

Name: _____

    Request: _____

Name: _____

    Request: _____

Name: _____

    Request: _____

Name: _____

    Request: _____

Name: _____

    Request: _____

Name: _____

    Request: _____

Name: _____

    Request: _____

Name: _____

    Request: _____

God Can!

Use this page and the next to keep a dated record of your prayer requests and God's responses to them.

DATE	I ASK GOD	HE ANSWERS	DATE

DATE	I ASK GOD	HE ANSWERS	DATE